W9-CHL-012

PLACE IN RETURN BOX to remove this checkout from your record.
TO AVOID FINES return on or before date due.
MAY BE RECALLED with earlier due date if requested.

DATE DUE	DATE DUE	DATE DUE
AUG 0 6 2013		
0 6 0 1 13		

6/01 c:/CIRC/DateDue.p65-p.15

Increasing Multicultural Understanding

MULTICULTURAL ASPECTS OF COUNSELING SERIES

SERIES EDITOR
Paul Pedersen, Ph.D., *Syracuse University*

Multicultural Aspects of Counseling is a series of specific, practical books written to help counselors increase multicultural awareness, knowledge, and skill. Action oriented, the series emphasizes decision making, problem solving, and direct involvement by the reader in a multicultural environment. Culture, as applied to the series, is defined broadly to include ethnographic, status, and affiliation variables. Counseling is also defined broadly, recognizing that in some cultures counseling uses less formal styles and methods. Authors are recognized authorities in their fields and/or at the cutting edge of new and innovative approaches for multicultural counseling from non-Western and Western perspectives.

EDITORIAL BOARD

Increasing Multicultural Understanding

A Comprehensive Model

Don C. Locke

Multicultural Aspects of Counseling Series 1

SAGE Publications
International Educational and Professional Publisher
Newbury Park   London   New Delhi

For information address:

SAGE Publications, Inc.
2455 Teller Road
Newbury Park, California 91320

SAGE Publications Ltd.
6 Bonhill Street
London EC2A 4PU
United Kingdom

SAGE Publications India Pvt. Ltd.
M-32 Market
Greater Kailash I
New Delhi 110 048 India

Printed in the United States of America

Library of Congress Cataloging-in-Publication Data

Locke, Don C.
    Increasing multicultural understanding: a comprehensive model /
Don C. Locke.
        p.   cm.—(Multicultural aspects of counseling; v. 1)
    Includes bibliographical references and index.
    ISBN 0-8039-4593-0 (cl).—ISBN 0-8039-4594-9 (pb)
    1. Pluralism (Social sciences)—United States. 2. Minorities—
United States. 3. United States—Ethnic relations. 4. United
States—Race relations. I. Title. II. Series.
E184.A1L63   1992
305.8′00973—dc20   92-17345

92 93 94 95 10 9 8 7 6 5 4 3 2 1

Sage Production Editor: Diane S. Foster

Contents

Dedication

To Tonya Elizabeth and Regina Camille

Acknowledgments

I am indebted to many people whose help, support, and advice has been invaluable in writing this book. First let me thank Fay Bostic and the counselor education faculty at North Carolina State University who supported a department head by functioning on "automatic pilot" while I was engaged with this project. The staff at the D. H. Hill Library at North Carolina State University was helpful in so many ways with the research necessary for the accuracy of this effort. Marquita Flemming and the Sage Publications staff made the effort an easy one as they directed the process from conception to completion.

The students in my classes, especially Marie Faubert, Larry Parker, and Sandy Peace contributed directly or indirectly to the fine tuning of my ideas and thoughts. I am deeply appreciative of their support throughout the process of trying to do justice to the various cultural groups.

I wish to express my appreciation to Allen Ivey who read an early draft of the manuscript and made helpful suggestions. Paul Pedersen, Series Editor, took this project under his supervision and directed it to conclusion. For their helpful suggestions, I am particularly indebted to the reviewers: Augustine Baron, University of Texas, Austin; Rita Chi-Ying Chung, University of California, Los Angeles; Mary Fukuyama, University of Florida; Roger Herring, Mapelvale, Little Rock, Arkansas; Evelyn Kalibala, New York Board of Education; Johnnie McFadden, University of South Carolina;

Jeff Mio, Washington State University; Satsuki Tomine, California State University; and Joe Whittmer, University of Florida.

Special thanks goes to my spouse, Marjorie, for being there in every way.

Series Editor's Introduction

This volume by Professor Donald Locke is the first volume in a new series of Sage books titled the "Multicultural Aspects of Counseling" (MAC) series. The MAC series of books was designed to fill a need for specific, practical, and less expensive books on selected aspects of multicultural counseling. The books in this series will focus on a specific population, method/strategy, or problem from a multicultural perspective so that each book might be used for teaching or personal development of multicultural counselors. Locke presents a very useful and practical model for examining complex cultural relationships in a systematic way.

The series is focused on practical issues that go beyond the rhetoric about multiculturalism, although it may include volumes on theories that can be applied to making changes in a multicultural environment. There will be an action orientation in the series that emphasizes decision making, problem solving, and direct involvement by the reader in a multicultural environment. Locke provides a practical tool in this volume for planning specific changes with specific cultural groups in an efficient way.

Culture, as applied to this series, is defined broadly rather than narrowly. That means that in addition to ethnographic variables (nationality, ethnicity, language, religion, etc.) the series may also focus on demographic variables (age, gender, place of residence, etc.) status variables (social, economic, educational, etc.) and affiliation variables (formal groups as well as informal groups). Any of these many social system variables may become the salient culture of reference for a client at any given point in time. Locke's book applies his model to nine different ethnic groups demonstrating *both* the similarities *and* the differences across these groups.

Although the series is conceptualized from a psychological perspective, the volumes in the series will be written from the perspective of other disciplines as well. There is a need to emphasize interdisciplinary cooperation in managing problems which cross over the boundaries of each discipline. The series will attempt to identify new and innovative approaches for multicultural counseling from non-Western as well as Western cultural perspectives. There is a need to identify alternatives for the traditional functions of counseling as they have been developed outside the Euro-American context. In his emphasis on *diversity* of both method and content, Locke points out the importance of multiple perspectives in counseling.

The series will define counseling broadly also, recognizing that in some cultures counseling uses less formal methods and/or takes place in less formal settings. There is a need to increase a counselor's repertoire of counseling styles to meet the needs of culturally different client populations. These styles might include teaching, training, or purposive conversation in an office, on a street corner, or at any other culturally appropriate location. In his epilogue, Locke points out an especially valuable series of principles and guidelines for implementing multicultural counseling through informal as well as formal approaches.

The series will emphasize an educational model, where the client is viewed as a student, more than the medical model where the client is viewed as a patient. The target population may be healthy—from within its own cultural perspective—rather than sick, even though that population deviates from the established norms of the dominant culture. In his introduction to the book Locke emphasizes the importance of educational solutions to multicultural problems as the single most promising hope for the future.

The series is designed to increase a reader's multicultural *awareness* through challenging culturally biased assumptions; *knowledge,* through presenting factual knowledge and information about a particular method, population or problem; and *skill* through identifying right actions based on appropriate awareness and accurate knowledge. Locke reaffirms this three step developmental sequence throughout his book guiding the reader toward a higher level of competence and effectiveness.

Locke's book is the beginning and not the end of your education as a multicultural counselor. The reader will almost certainly disagree at points with what is being said on this most controversial topic. This book will not give you all the answers, but it will guide you toward the sources you need in finding those answers for yourself.

Paul Pedersen
Syracuse University

Introduction: A Blueprint for Multicultural Understanding

We are living in an age of diversity. The role of teachers and counselors has been expanded to include the consideration of the cultural identities of students and clients. Teachers and counselors have a responsibility to increase their awareness, knowledge, and skills so that all students and clients are taught and counseled with approaches that recognize the influences of cultural group membership. If teachers and counselors do not recognize the influence of cultural group membership, students and clients can be expected to profit only minimally from our interactions with them.

This book sets forth, one brick at a time, the process necessary to implement effective education and counseling strategies for culturally diverse populations. Helping culturally different students and clients requires a focus of effort for each student or client based on both individual needs and cultural group membership needs.

This book is designed to provide one of the necessary steps in accomplishing the task of gaining an overview of cultural groups. It will help the reader identify characteristics of cultures, make comparisons between the dominant culture and the culturally different groups, make comparisons among culturally different groups, and use that information to develop strategies or interventions for students or clients. The book is designed to help make readers aware of their own ethnocentrism and to increase their awareness of the role culture plays in determining the ways people think, feel, and act.

Multiculturalism has been described as a fourth force in psychology. As we prepare to enter the twenty-first century, we are confronted with the demand for attention to diverse populations in education and counseling. The crisis in the United States today results from the alienation experienced by culturally different individuals and groups. The "melting pot" theory of assimilation appears to have been rejected by members of the dominant culture as well as by members of culturally different populations. More and more people are accepting the pluralistic nature of the culture of the United States. The methods of dealing with people who are different must be amended to provide for people's unique needs based on their own unique cultural group characteristics. We can no longer accept a singular method of teaching or counseling as useful for all our students or clients. We can no longer accept theories of teaching or counseling that do not include a focus that is broad enough to be applicable to students and clients who are different from the dominant viewpoint in education and counseling. The fourth force requires that we attend to needs of students and clients that may not be consistent with the predominant viewpoint of our professional training.

We must revise our educational practices and counseling strategies in a broad way. How and why have the experiences of culturally different groups been similar to and different from one another? How and why have the experiences of culturally different groups been similar to and different from those of the dominant culture? To answer these questions, we must not only study statistics about groups, we must ask the culturally different to write their own histories. We need to know what is on the minds of individuals from culturally different populations. While we know that culturally different individuals and groups all face obstacles in the United States that are similar, and that they all face similar issues related to acculturation, the key to understanding a particular cultural group lies in an appreciation of the wide diversity of the individuals' experiences.

The model of multicultural understanding presented in this book has been designed to provide teachers and counselors with information that, when combined with the pedagogy of the profession, will enable the users to be better able to provide for the needs of all students or clients. The model is designed to provide no more than a basic foundation for teaching or counseling. It does not attempt to answer all questions that might emerge about a particular cultural group. The model should serve as a beginning for more in-depth study of a particular cultural group. It is a springboard for understanding the cultures included in this volume, and should be used with caution. Those who believe that the model is all-inclusive will soon discover that it is virtually impossible for any model or scheme to be so comprehensive that no additional information will be needed.

The elements selected for inclusion in the model are those that appeared to be most relevant for use across cultures. Some elements are more useful and important in one culture than in others. For some elements it was difficult to force the cultural group information to fit the model. For others, there appeared to be a natural fit of the information on the cultural group with the model. In all cases the model was used as the basis for providing information on the particular cultural group.

Each chapter was written with a clear understanding that cultures are heterogeneous and that any attempt at generalization about a particular cultural group is dangerous. Readers are reminded to treat the information with caution. Students in a multicultural counseling course have used the material and have provided their critiques. Also, each chapter was submitted to a member of the cultural group discussed in that chapter for a blind review. Revisions were made based on the recommendations of these reviewers.

Teachers and counselors must acknowledge that all individuals are, in some respects, like all other individuals. All individuals are members of the human race, and, as such, share many characteristics. All individuals share membership in our own species, *Homo sapiens.*

All individuals are, in some respects, like some other individuals, as a result of cultural group membership. The cultural group serves as the basis for individuals to become humanized. Each individual becomes fully human through the process of participating in a cultural group or groups.

All individuals are, in some respects, like no other individuals, in that there is some uniqueness in each individual. Individuals differ from one another both biologically and socially. No two individuals share the same experiences in their society.

What these three identities mean for teachers and counselors is that they must be aware that each individual is seeking a personal identity, to a greater or lesser degree, by acknowledging an identity with a cultural group while living in a world community. By acknowledging the influences of cultural group membership on personal identity, teachers and counselors increasingly heighten their sensitivity to and awareness of issues related to the success of each student or client.

Each chapter in this volume is divided into an introduction, a discussion of the 10 elements from the model, implications for education and/or counseling, questions for review and reflection, and references. Taken as a whole, each chapter presents my interpretation of what I consider the most important and useful information on the cultural group discussed. In no way is the material presented here to be considered exhaustive of information about any particular cultural group. Readers who wish more detailed knowledge about a particular group are encouraged to begin with the references at the end of the appropriate chapter and then seek additional information from other sources.

This book is intended for undergraduate or graduate courses in multicultural education or counseling. It can be used as a supplement to a text for a course in which the instructor wants students to have specific information on a number of cultural groups.

Controversy is likely to be one product of this book. Since there is no consensus about what constitutes relevant cultural group information, whether certain facts are historically or currently relevant, the degree of homogeneity among cultural group members, and what methods are best for interventions with culturally different populations, some readers may disagree with what I have written about some cultural groups. The controversy will be useful if it leads to a clearer understanding of cultural groups and how best to provide for their educational and counseling needs.

1

A Model of Multicultural Understanding

The model of multicultural understanding presented in this volume is a comprehensive model that can be used as a guide to gain knowledge and understanding of culturally diverse individuals and groups. This knowledge and understanding can then be reflected appropriately in educational and/or counseling situations. The model was designed to include all the elements of personal awareness and information necessary for a person to engage in positive and productive relationships with culturally diverse individuals or groups. It is useful for teachers, individual counselors, family counselors, and those involved in any intervention within culturally diverse communities.

The model (Figure 1.1) provides a solid, sound foundation for exploring ethnic differences. While thorough and comprehensive, it is succinct enough to be useful in examining the cultural patterns, social relationships, and experiences of culturally diverse individuals and groups.

Self-Awareness

One uses the model by beginning with self-awareness. This component refers to the traditional "know thyself" element of Greek philosophy. In helping relationships with the culturally diverse it might be necessary and useful for those involved to share their personal experiences. Knowing one's own

1

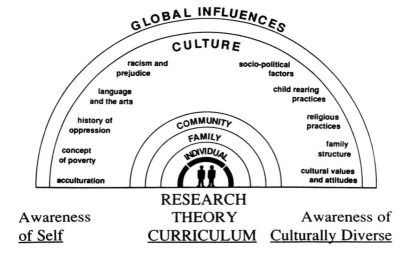

Figure 1.1. Multicultural Understanding

personal biases, values, and interests—which stem from culture—as well as one's own culture will greatly enhance one's sensitivity toward other cultures. Awareness of self is the first step to understanding others (Locke, 1986); in seeking that awareness, one might attempt to answer the following questions:

(1) What is my cultural heritage? What was the culture of my parents and my grandparents? With what cultural group(s) do I identify?

(2) What is the cultural relevance of my name?

(3) What values, beliefs, opinions, and attitudes do I hold that are consistent with the dominant culture? Which are inconsistent? How did I learn these?

(4) How did I decide to become a teacher or counselor? What cultural standards were involved in the process? What do I understand to be the relationship between culture and education and/or counseling?

(5) What unique abilities, aspirations, expectations, and limitations do I have that might influence my relations with culturally diverse individuals?

Global Influences

What happens in our world today often becomes more meaningful if where it happens has some relevance at a personal level. The culturally sensitive individual must be cognizant of world events and how members of various cultures translate those events into personal meaning. The world is becoming smaller and smaller, and events in a cultural group's country of origin may produce significant emotional reactions in group members. Some culturally diverse individuals may have relatives who still live in their countries of origin and may be quite sensitive to events in those countries, the policies of the U.S. government toward those events, and the attitudes of helpers toward them. Such interest on the part of culturally diverse individuals necessitates some knowledge of world affairs. Shifts in the economic and political scenes in the United States greatly influence the state of affairs in South America, Africa, and Asia. Knowledge of the culture in a client's country of origin provides the helper with a more complete picture of that client's worldview.

Dominant Culture

This model uses the general culture of the United States as the backdrop for understanding culturally diverse individuals and groups. The model is useful in any setting where there are two reasonably different cultural groups. It seems appropriate for teachers and counselors to have a fairly clear knowledge of the values of the dominant culture.

Fairchild (1970) defines *culture* as "all behavior patterns socially acquired and socially transmitted by means of symbols," including customs, techniques, beliefs, institutions, and material objects (p. 80). The primary mode of transmission of culture is language, which enables people to learn, experience, and share their traditions and customs.

Steward (1972) identifies five components of culture in his summary of cultural assumptions and values:

(1) *Activity:* How do people approach activity? How important are goals in life? Who makes decisions? What is the nature of problem solving?

(2) *Definition of social relations:* How are roles defined? How do people relate to those whose status is different? How are sex roles defined? What is the meaning of friendship?

(3) *Motivation:* What is the achievement orientation of the culture? Is cooperation or competition emphasized?

(4) *Perception of the world:* What is the predominant worldview? What is the predominant view on human nature? What is the predominant view on the nature of truth? How is time defined? What is the nature of property?

(5) *Perception of self and the individual:* How is self defined? Where is a person's identity determined? What is the nature of the individual? What kinds of persons are valued and respected?

Robin M. Williams, Jr. (1970), a noted sociologist, has identified 15 cultural themes and orientations that generally reflect the Anglo-Saxon influence on the culture of the United States. While not all Anglo-Saxons value these themes/orientations, they nevertheless reflect what many determine to be predominant in the culture of the United States. Noted historian John Hope Franklin (as cited in Fersh, 1978) has concluded that by the end of the nineteenth century, American standards of ethnicity accepted Anglo-Saxons as the norm, placed other whites on what might be called "ethnic probation," and excluded all others from serious consideration. Thus it seems logical to describe Anglo-Saxon values as representative of the culture of the United States. The themes and orientations identified by Williams are as follows:

(1) *Achievement and success:* There is an emphasis on rags-to-riches success stories.

(2) *Activity and work:* This is a land of busy people who stress disciplined, productive activity as a worthy end in itself.

(3) *Humanitarian mores:* People spontaneously come to the aid of others and hold traditional sympathy for the "underdog."

(4) *Moral orientation:* Life events and situations are judged in terms of right and wrong.

(5) *Efficiency and practicality:* There is an emphasis on the practical value of getting things done.

(6) *Progress:* An optimistic view is held that things will get better.

(7) *Material comfort:* Emphasis is placed on the good life. Many are conspicuous consumers.

(8) *Equality:* There is a constant avowal of the commitment to equality.

(9) *Freedom:* The belief in individual freedom takes on almost a religious connotation.

(10) *External conformity:* There is great uniformity in matters of dress, housing, recreation, manners, and even the expression of political ideas.

(11) *Science and secular rationality:* There is esteem for the sciences as a means of asserting mastery over the environment.

(12) *Nationalism-patriotism:* There exists a strong sense of loyalty to that which is called "American."

(13) *Democracy:* There is a belief that every person should have a voice in the political destiny of the country.

(14) *Individual personality:* Every individual should be independent, responsible, and self-respecting. The group should not take precedence over the individual.

(15) *Racism and related group superiority:* This theme represents the chief value conflict in the culture of the United States, because it emphasizes differential evaluation of racial, religious, and ethnic groups.

One must understand the dominant culture from the perspectives of the individual, the family, and the community. We need to know how that culture defines a psychologically healthy individual, reinforces the family for its acculturation function, and defines the concept of community in terms of size and who is included in it.

Cultural Differences

In the model, there are many elements of the culture to examine. There are sociopolitical factors, the culture's history of oppression, the experience of prejudice and racism, poverty within the culture, influence of language and the arts, influence of religious practices, child-rearing practices, family role and structure, values and attitudes, and the degree of opposition to acculturation. This model is similar to Sue and Sue's (1990) model in that they stress the impact of sociocultural forces as well as the psychological and developmental influences on the behavioral expressions of different racial and ethnic groups.

Thus as immigrants come to the United States they are influenced by the existing environmental conditions. They have brought with them their own psychological and behavioral qualities, including language and the arts, child-rearing practices, religious practices, family structure, and values and attitudes. These two sets of factors work either against each other or together to form and shape the new immigrant into a participant in the culture of the United States. The "Americanization" process is designed to blend the many ethnic ingredients so that one nationality is produced. The degree to which an immigrant group is assimilated into the culture of the United States occurs by mutual consent. For some, the dominant culture resists assimilation. For others, the immigrant group itself elects to remain outside the main cultural group. Under either circumstance, the gap that exists between the dominant culture and the immigrants' culture of origin is likely to present major problems for helping professionals from the dominant culture who do not have knowledge about and sensitivity to culturally diverse individuals or groups.

The model allows for scrutiny of the following 10 cultural elements: degree of acculturation, poverty, history of oppression, language and the arts, racism and prejudice, sociopolitical factors, child-rearing practices, religious practices, family structure, and values and attitudes. When investigating these 10 cultural elements to find out about a particular cultural group, one must remember that there are differences *within* cultural groups that may be greater than the differences between the dominant culture and other cultures. Helping professionals must bear in mind that the uniqueness of the individual must, at all times, be respected along with the uniqueness of the cultural group. Giving too much attention to the individual encourages neglect of the impact of the cultural group on the individual. Giving too much attention to the cultural group runs the risk of stereotyping the individual as a member of that cultural group and forgetting individual uniqueness. The helper must keep both the individual's uniqueness and the cultural group membership foremost in mind as he or she works with the culturally diverse.

Following are brief discussions of the 10 elements of the model. I believe these represent the most important elements, in terms of knowledge about and sensitivity toward other cultures, for counselors and other helping professionals to understand.

Acculturation

As stated earlier, the members of any given cultural group are not all alike. One major difference among members of various cultural groups is the degree to which they have immersed themselves in the culture of the United States. Members of culturally diverse groups might be classified as (a) *bicultural,* able to function as effectively in the dominant culture as in their own, while holding on to manifestations of their own culture; (b) *traditional,* holding on to a majority of cultural traits from the culture of origin while rejecting many of the traits of the dominant culture; (c) *marginal,* having little real contact with traits of either culture; or (d) *acculturated,* having given up most of the cultural traits of the culture of origin and assumed the traits of the dominant culture. When looking at the degree of acculturation, one might also seek to determine at what level(s) individuals belonging to culturally diverse groups have acculturated in terms of marital, attitudinal, behavioral, civic, structural, and identification factors.

The helping professional from the dominant culture must have a clear understanding that there is a natural tendency on the part of many members of culturally diverse groups to resist acculturation. The helper needs to understand that this resistance is not personal, and that some of the resistance is based on nothing more than the time the individual has lived in the dominant culture. Other resistance is a genuine rejection of the cultural values perpetuated by the general culture. Thus the culturally diverse may be identified by the unique cultural values commonly held within their cultural group.

Poverty and Economic Concerns

Persons living below the poverty level in the United States include inordinate numbers of ethnic/racial culture group members. The effective helper of culturally diverse individuals or groups has a clear view as to why poverty exists within a society. Knowledge of the historic causes of poverty, the political and economic factors that perpetuate poverty, and the networking being carried out in the client's local community to eradicate poverty will enhance the ability of the culturally sensitive helper to work with culturally diverse individuals. Factors such as housing, employment, educational opportunity, and life expectancy are often clearly associated with poverty among members of culturally diverse populations.

Some might even argue that discrimination, prejudice, and racism, which express themselves differently in different countries, are more a reflection of economic status than of racial or ethnic group membership. Helpers need to have empathy for poor people. Good helpers have a repertoire of strategies to recommend that include alternatives to the traditional dominant culture's view of poverty and how to overcome it.

History of Oppression

Educators cannot explore only those factors relating to individuals' experiences in the present. They must understand and have empathy for those events from the past or future that have an impact on the present. Likewise, while there is much evidence that the history of culturally diverse groups in the United States often is unpleasant, educators must be willing to explore this unpleasant material so that culturally diverse individuals can better deal with events in the present. For some culturally diverse persons, it is a recollection of the past or even the reading of history that contributes to their willingness or unwillingness to interact with the dominant culture. Teachers and counselors must explore what this actual or vicarious oppression has done to the psychological adjustment of culturally diverse students or clients.

Language and the Arts

A major question exists within the dominant culture regarding how much the culture should tolerate those who do not speak "Standard English." Since it appears that the dominant culture wishes the culturally diverse to acculturate, and since language is the means by which culture is transmitted, it seems logical that the dominant culture would desire that all persons learn the language as soon as possible. The ability to speak Standard English thus becomes a symbolic measure by which members of culturally diverse groups are often judged. Little attention is given to fostering bilingualism, and many hold contempt for individuals whose spoken language or dialect is noticeably different from Standard English.

Likewise, similar emotions are generated regarding art or art forms. For example, the standard artistic form of the dominant culture in the United States is linear, with a progressive organization that drives toward climax, catharsis, and closure. The artistic forms prevalent in many culturally diverse groups place heavy emphasis on circular organization, involvement through repetition of sound and movement, and short units leading to a succession of mini-climaxes. African-American audiences interact with a performer through a great deal of "call and response." The better known and respected the performer, the greater the response. On the other hand, dominant-culture audiences in the United States indicate their approval of an artistic expression through silence, quiet attention, and mild response to the performer. The greatest sign of approval is given at the conclusion of the performance.

Significant attention should be given to nonverbal communication as well. Helping professionals need to know that culture determines such elements of communication as tone of voice, rate of speech, pitch, volume, proxemics, haptics, kinesics, smiling, occulism, and greetings and farewells. Albert Mehrabian (1981) has concluded that in any given total message, 7% of the communication is verbal, 38% is vocal, and 55% is facial. This demonstrates clearly the need for understanding and appreciation of nonverbal communication within the cultural context.

Racism and Prejudice

Prejudice is defined as judging before fully examining the object of evaluation. *Racial prejudice* refers to judgment based on racial/ethnic/cultural group membership before getting to know the person. *Racism* combines prejudice with power—power to do something based on prejudiced beliefs.

In our urgency to categorize people, we all use some prior knowledge in the process. Thus all people are prejudiced. Prejudice may be personal, institutional, or cultural. Personal prejudice includes beliefs about individuals as part of a particular group. Institutional prejudice is prejudice that has been incorporated into the structure of an institution based on the beliefs of the people who have influenced the institution. Cultural prejudice, or ethnocentrism, is demonstrated in an assertion of a cultural group's superiority in accomplishments, creativity, or achievements.

One way to understand prejudice and racism is through the use of a matrix that views the expression of prejudice/racism along two dimensions: overt versus covert, and intentional versus unintentional (Locke & Hardaway, 1980). The matrix yields four types of prejudice/racism:

(1) *overt intentional:* openly espousing a doctrine of inferiority of culturally diverse groups
(2) *overt unintentional:* counseling culturally diverse clients toward lower socioeconomic status jobs/careers
(3) *covert intentional:* expecting culturally diverse individuals to communicate nonverbally exactly as do members of the dominant culture
(4) *covert unintentional:* explicitly identifying the races of members of particular cultures when certain behaviors are described

Racism and prejudice are inextricably entwined in the oppression of culturally diverse groups in the United States. From the moment white Europeans first stepped onto the soil of the Atlantic coast, attitudes of superiority and lack of understanding of other cultural group members have been predominant. Many of those attitudes persist today, and many have been absorbed into the training and education of counselors and other helping professionals. Helping professionals have an opportunity and a responsibility to communicate honestly and directly regarding the views they hold about culturally diverse groups.

Terry (1970) describes six attitudes/beliefs/behaviors of dominant group members who wish to be positive influences with culturally diverse populations: Dominant group members must move beyond guilt, value the self-worth of persons, understand power, take risks, be proactive, and value pluralism. Adherence to these principles should enhance the attractiveness of dominant-culture members who work with persons who are culturally different from themselves.

Sociopolitical Factors

Helping professionals need to understand the culturally unique social factors that affect a culture. Many items in this category overlap other areas (e.g., family structure, child-rearing practices), but others are quite different. The celebration of holidays, the roles of social organizations, and how friendship is determined are all examples of social factors that are unique within cultural groups.

Political factors include the area of self-determination within the cultural group. The level of involvement in the political process at local, state, and national levels may be a function of the dominant culture's imposing restrictions as well as the degree of interest and belief in the political system as an avenue for group advancement.

Child-Rearing Practices

The family is the primary socialization agent of a culture, and thus the process of child rearing itself can be very revealing of a culture's structure and values. By examining specific child-rearing practices in a culture, one can learn much about kinship networks, how sex roles are socialized, how respect is taught, who is respected, when children are taught to be assertive, obligations of children to parents and of parents to children, and the place of competition in the culture.

Religious Practices

Religion is an organized system of the belief in a god, gods, or other supernatural beings. Religion helps a cultural group determine relationships with other peoples and with the universe. In some cultural groups religion and local politics are closely tied. Some cultural protest organizations had their beginnings in religious organizations. For some cultural groups, religion has been a primary source of strength for coping with the demands of the dominant culture. For others, religion has been the primary determinant of a sense of community, providing a basis for cohesion and moral strength within the cultural group.

Family Structure and Dynamics

The family, the oldest human institution, is the basic unit of a culture. The family is responsible for the production of children who will continue the culture, as well as for the socialization of those children. The manner in which the culture organizes itself in kinship patterns provides useful information on its structure. Factors such as who has authority in families and in what areas, the impact of marriage outside the cultural group, the nature of relationships among members of the family, and how lineage is determined are useful in understanding the impact of family structure on the culture.

Cultural Values and Attitudes

Kluckhorn and Strodtbeck (1961) provide five categories of questions that are useful in examining cultural values and attitudes:

(1) *Time:* Is the orientation based on the past, the present, or the future?
(2) *Human relations:* Are individuals, collateral relationships, or lineal relationships valued most?

(3) *Human activity:* Is the focus on doing, being, or becoming?

(4) *Human nature:* At birth, are people considered basically good, bad, neutral, or mixed?

(5) *Supernatural:* Is the relationship with the supernatural one of control, subordination, or harmony?

Research, Theory, and Curriculum

The 10 elements in the model, when related to culturally diverse groups, provide insight into specific research questions that may be investigated. Various assumptions of traditional educational and counseling theories may also be challenged and even altered to fit the specifics of members of culturally diverse populations. Curriculum modifications may be implemented, from elementary schools to graduate-level training, that reflect sensitivity to members of culturally diverse populations.

The nature of many culturally diverse groups limits their accessibility as communities, and therefore it is difficult to conduct direct research without being intrusive. However, important questions may be answered through observations, discussions, and participation of the researcher in the culture of the group under study. Research questions might focus on examination of the conditions under which members of culturally diverse groups seek assistance from members of the dominant culture. In the final analysis, however, this research is best conducted by professionals who are themselves members of the cultural groups under investigation.

From information obtained by examining the 10 elements in the model and derived from research, several considerations for educational and counseling theory emerge and require evaluation if useful and effective counseling strategies are to be developed for use with the culturally diverse. These areas include definitions of normality within the cultural group, the place of the individual within the system, how independence is treated within the culture, the place of support in the culture, and the meaning of personal change (Pedersen, 1987).

Often "normality" is judged by how much a person or group of individuals varies from the dominant culture in the larger society. Most educational and counseling theories are based on the assumption that a single standard is the norm by which all individuals should be judged. Given this rather narrowly focused assumption, culturally diverse individuals might be considered deviant with respect to socialization, religion, education, and other areas. Normality in a culturally diverse population must be considered within the context of the individual's subgroup and its own esoteric rules.

Although most theories of development in the United States are based on the assumption that the *individual* is the basic building block of society, this notion does not hold for many cultural groups. In many cultures, the family unit and, ultimately, the entire community operate as a strong bonding system that supports each individual. Considering the goals of an individual group member to be more important than group welfare might be offensive in a group-centered culture. In a similar vein, independence is viewed as "good" or "healthy" in the dominant culture of the United States, but among many other cultural populations, dependence on the family and/or the community is the accepted standard for survival.

To be effective in working with culturally diverse individuals, helping professionals must not use methods that advocate change for the sake of the system. For example, a person who is "leaving" his or her culture of origin should not be asked to give up all of his or her values in order to make the transition into the dominant culture.

After considering the 10 elements of culturally diverse populations addressed in the model and exploring specific research questions and implications for theory, it is possible to propose strategies for curriculum modification and change. Curriculum alterations are needed from the elementary level through the graduate level. Elementary school-age students can study various perspectives derived from many cultures. In schools with large concentrations of members of culturally diverse groups as students, or in communities where they live, specific attention needs to be directed to the study of these groups. Such programs should stress the positive aspects of these cultures, along with the principle of mutual respect for one another's cultural differences.

Curricula for college and graduate students, especially in teacher education and counselor education programs, should include the study of many cultures, with emphasis on appreciation of contributions of all groups to the society. Courses in areas such as multicultural education, multicultural counseling, and cross-cultural communication can serve to help students become aware of perspectives other than their own.

Summary

To meet the needs of culturally diverse populations, helping professionals who work with them must have an understanding of culturally consistent assessment, evaluation, and treatment skills, as well as theoretical content. The model of cross-cultural understanding presented above offers a framework for such action. This model does not specifically address skills; rather, it is meant to provide a foundation upon which counselors and educators can

build relationships with students and clients from culturally diverse populations, through the knowledge they gain from the study of culturally diverse
groups. Effective education and counseling of the culturally diverse can
occur only when teachers and counselors have knowledge of both educa-
tion/counseling theory and the particulars relevant to the individuals and
groups they are trying to help.

Questions for Review and Reflection

(1) Define the following terms:
culture
bicultural
marginal
culturally diverse
proxemics
kinesics
melting pot
prejudice
racism
acculturated

(2) Using the questions in the section on self-awareness, identify how you
have been influenced by your cultural background.

(3) What world events have had the greatest impact on your work as an
educator or counselor?

(4) Using Steward's (1972) summary of cultural assumptions and values,
explain what factors have influenced you most in the development of
your unique self.

(5) Which of Robin Williams's (1970) cultural themes appears most relevant to you personally? How has this cultural theme helped or hindered
your development as an educator or counselor?

(6) Which of the 10 elements used to describe culturally diverse groups do
you think is most important in your work? Why?

(7) How does the model help you as an educator or counselor understand
the importance of using culture-specific strategies/techniques with culturally diverse populations?

(8) Describe what might be called a "typical" person from the dominant
culture of the United States. How do you differ from this typical person?

(9) Identify and explain three major assumptions underlying the model
presented in this chapter.

(10) Explain some potential hazards inherent in sending inconsistent nonverbal messages.

(11) How does an acculturation viewpoint differ from a culturally diverse (pluralist) viewpoint in terms of the qualities necessary for success in the United States?

(12) What ethnic customs do you and your family practice? What values are represented in these customs?

References

Fairchild, H. P. (Ed.). (1970). *Dictionary of sociology and related sciences.* Totowa, NJ: Rowan & Allanheld.

Fersh, S. (1978). *Asia: Teaching about/learning from.* New York: Teachers College Press.

Kluckhorn, F., & Strodtbeck, F. (1961). *Variations in value orientations.* Evanston, IL: Row, Peterson.

Locke, D. C. (1986). Cross-cultural counseling issues. In A. J. Palmo & W. J. Weikel (Eds.), *Foundations of mental health counseling.* Springfield, IL: Charles C Thomas.

Locke, D. C., & Hardaway, Y. V. (1980). Moral perspectives in interracial settings. In D. Cochrane & M. Manley-Casimir (Eds.), *Moral education: Practical approaches.* (pp. 269-285). New York: Praeger.

Mehrabian, A. (1981). *Silent messages.* Belmont, CA: Wadsworth.

Pedersen, P. (1987). Ten frequent assumptions of cultural bias in counseling. *Journal of Multicultural Counseling and Development, 15,* 16-24.

Steward, E. C. (1972). *American cultural patterns.* La Grange Park, IL: Intercultural Network.

Sue, D. W., & Sue, D. (1990). *Counseling the culturally different: Theory and practice* (2nd ed.). New York: John Wiley.

Terry, R. W. (1970). *For whites only.* Grand Rapids, MI: Eerdmans.

Williams, R. M., Jr. (1970). *American society: A sociological interpretation.* New York: Knopf.

2

African Americans

Since coming to the United States from Africa, black Americans' experiences have been paradoxical: hardship and uncertainty on the one hand, and accomplishment and determination on the other. The institution of slavery, followed by emancipation, with its sanctioned institutional arrangements of political, social, and economic segregation and discrimination, produced a people who provide the greatest challenge to the democratic principles of the dominant culture's emphasis and focus on equality and egalitarianism.

The African-American population, currently the largest culturally different group in the United States, has undergone some significant changes over the course of its history in terms of growth, distribution, and composition. At the time the first census of the United States was taken in 1790, there were about 757,000 African Americans in the country. By 1980, there were 26.4 million African Americans in the United States. Prior to World War II, three of every four African Americans lived in the South. By 1970, 81% of African Americans lived in urban areas, and only 50% lived in the South.

Throughout this chapter the term *African American* is used because it is consistent with terms used to describe other groups. It is also used because the term *black* is inadequate to convey the rich history of the peoples who came to the United States from the continent of Africa. For most of the history of African Americans in the United States, there has been a tendency to omit the history of this group in Africa and to begin the history as of the time the first Africans

15

arrived in the New World in 1619. *African American* is used also because the term *black* has been associated with darkness, evil, and ignorance, while the term *white* has been associated with brightness, good, and intelligence.

Acculturation

Valentine (1971) believes that most of the African-American community is bicultural. He concludes that the collective behavior and social life of the African-American community is bicultural in the sense that each African-American ethnic segment draws upon both a distinctive repertoire of standardized African-American behaviors and, simultaneously, patterns derived from the dominant culture. Socialization into both systems begins at an early age and continues throughout life, and both systems are generally of equal importance in most individuals' lives.

Pinderhughes (1989) describes a meeting with a group of teachers in which one teacher had this to say about the bicultural condition:

> A mother explained when I was questioning her values about allowing him to fight, "I'll take care of his behavior; you take care of his education. Where we live he has to be tough and be able to fight. I'm not going to stop that. You set your standards here and see that he understands he has to abide by them." (p. 181)

Staples (1976) suggests that the bicultural nature of African Americans is something forced upon them and is often antithetical to their own values. He goes on to say that the commitment to Eurocentric values is not necessarily positive, and that although African Americans may engage in Euro-American cultural practices—such as individualism and materialism—this should not be taken as a strong commitment to those values.

Essien-Udoms's (1962) concept of the dilemma of duality suggests that African Americans must choose to act either "the black way" or "the nonblack way." The dilemma is resolved when African Americans distinguish between themselves and their "role."

Myrdal (1944) concludes that "it is to the advantage of American Negroes as individuals and as a group to become assimilated into American culture, to acquire the traits held in esteem by the dominant white culture" (p. 929).

Poverty and Economic Concerns

Historically, African-American unemployment rates have been at least twice those of the members of the dominant culture (Dovidio & Gaertner,

1986). Many reasons have been given for this phenomenon, among them that African Americans have a higher turnover rate in jobs, and that many of the jobs filled by African Americans are short term to begin with.

C. Young (1986, p. 63) concludes that African-American poverty levels are, to some extent, due to the following factors: the scarcity of jobs in central cities, the fact that African-American women tend to have children at younger ages, the widening gap between African-American and white unemployment rates, racial discrimination, and the large increase in the number of white females in the labor force.

Billingsley (1968) has noted that even when income levels are similar for African Americans and members of the dominant culture, the two groups are not comparable. This is so because the African-American group must reflect its experience with job discrimination and racism, both of which set the conditions for growing up African American in the United States.

By 1970, almost four-fifths of the African-American population lived in the nation's central cities, with 31% of the total African-American population living on incomes below the official poverty line. Malveaux (1988) reports that income distribution has changed for African Americans in three ways since 1970: (a) the proportion of African Americans in poverty has increased, (b) the proportion of African Americans with incomes between $15,000 and $34,999 has declined, and (c) the proportion of African Americans at the highest income levels (more than $35,000) has risen by almost a third.

Swinton (1983) characterizes the economic plight of African Americans thus:

> Blacks have consistently experienced a relatively disadvantageous labor market position in good times and bad. Black workers typically have higher rates of unemployment, obtain fewer high paying jobs, more low paying jobs, and have lower wage rates than whites. The combination of obtaining less work and lower paid work results, as we have seen, in blacks obtaining significantly smaller amount of income from labor than whites. (p. 62)

Between 1970 and 1980, the median income of African-American families had decreased from $13,325 to $12,674, while median income for whites rose from $21,722 to $21,904 for the same period (U.S. Department of Commerce, Bureau of the Census, 1980).

Traditionally, African Americans experience higher rates of joblessness, underemployment, mortality, morbidity, family instability, poor housing, homicide, and institutionalization than their white counterparts. There is no greater issue facing African Americans than the economic one.

History of Oppression

African Americans were enslaved and subjected to a system of bondage with few parallels in human history. Formal slavery ended following the Civil War, and a social system developed that continued to relegate the former slaves and their descendants to a position of inferiority in the dominant culture. This oppressed status has been recognized as a major social problem with current ramifications in all categories of the lives of African Americans.

Racism is still the dominant force in the United States insofar as attitudes and behavior toward African Americans are concerned. Changes in the status of African Americans have occurred, but the lack of significant change in the first 100 years after emancipation had the effect of compounding the problems. Racism sustains and reinforces the privileges that members of the dominant culture enjoy, thereby maintaining the dominant culture and oppressing African Americans.

Hale-Benson (1982) found that even the literary treatment of slavery by the dominant culture has influenced the view that African Americans have of themselves. She recommends the following:

> We need an extensive investigation of the acculturative process and the reaction of Black people to enslavement and slave status. The traditional interpretation of Black history has emphasized the acquiescence of Blacks to slavery. Recognizing the resistance to slavery is important because slaves who acquiesced in their status would be more prone to accept the culture of their masters than those who rebelled. Similarly, if they were reluctant to accept slave status, they would have struggled harder to retain what they could of their African culture and heritage. (pp. 12-13)

Many of the differences between the primary social institutions in the African-American community and in the dominant culture are a result of the long history of oppression. While there have been changes in the twentieth century, the racism of the dominant culture and the African-American consciousness will promote the distinctive aspects within the social institutions.

In a classic study, Myrdal (1944, pp. 60-61) developed the following rank order of types of segregation and discrimination against African Americans:

(1) the bar against intermarriage and sexual intercourse involving white women
(2) discrimination specifically concerning behavior in personal relations (barriers against the races dancing, bathing, eating, or drinking together, and social intermingling generally)

(3) segregation and discrimination in use of public facilities such as schools, churches, and means of conveyance
(4) political disenfranchisement
(5) discrimination in law courts, by the police, and by other public servants
(6) discrimination in securing land, credit, jobs, or other means of earning a living, and discrimination in public relief and other social welfare activities

It is important to note that African Americans in the Myrdal study ranked their concerns with the areas of segregation and discrimination in a parallel, but inverse, order. Likewise, it is interesting to note that the items in the discrimination rankings for more than 50 years ago remain today as issues separating African Americans from the dominant culture. Such a pattern of relations results in the isolation of African Americans from members of the dominant culture, and vice versa, and this isolation provides the opportunity for stereotypes to persist as significant racial issues.

Language and the Arts

There are two major positions concerning the spoken language of African Americans. The language deficit position posited by Deutsch (1965) holds that the lack of appropriate early language stimulation in African-American homes results in immature or deficient language development. Those who adhere to this position believe that the speech patterns of African-American children are incorrect and must be corrected according to the linguistic rules of Standard English.

Linguists such as Baratz (1969) and Smitherman (1977), on the other hand, take the position that all human beings develop some form of language and contend that African Americans employ a well-ordered, highly structured, highly developed language system that in many aspects is different from Standard English. Although Black English is similar to Standard English in many respects, it is different from Standard English in its phonological and grammatical structure. Smitherman (1977) concludes:

> African slaves in America initially developed a pidgin, a language of transaction, that was used in communication between themselves and whites. Over the years, the pidgin gradually became widespread among slaves and evolved into a Creole. Developed without benefit of any formal instruction, this lingo involved the substitution of English for West African words, but within the same basic structure and idiom that characterized West African language patterns. (p. 5)

Smitherman identifies some of the West African language rules that still operate in Black English today. Included among the grammar and structural rules are the repetition of the noun subject with the pronoun ("My father, he work there"), question patterns without the verb *to do* ("What it come to?"), and an emphasis on the character of action without the tense indicated in the verb ("I know it good when he ask me"). West African sound rules that are found in Black English include no consonant pairs ("jus" for "just"), no *r* sound ("mo" for "more"), and no *th* sound ("souf" for "south").

Black English appears to be maintained by social pressures within the African-American community, although the speakers are often unaware that they are maintaining it. Group identity provides a strong subconscious pressure to maintain the dialect even while the speaker's conscious effort may be to speak Standard English. Among some groups, especially writers, speaking Black English has become a symbol of African-American unity.

A number of researchers have identified a unique cultural form that is expressed in African-American arts. Hale-Benson (1982) characterizes the African-American style as circular, with a "heavy emphasis on involvement through repetition of sound and movement," with an "episodic arrangement calling for small, short units leading to a succession of mini-climaxes" (p. 41). There is also a tendency to retreat from closure in favor of the ongoing and open-ended.

Racism and Prejudice

The issue of race and racism is one that has engaged a great deal of attention and has preoccupied many as it relates to African Americans in the United States. W. E. B. Du Bois (1961) noted in 1910, with particular reference to race relations between the dominant culture and African Americans, that "the problem of the Twentieth Century is the problem of the colorline" (p. 41).

It is evident that the Anglo-Saxon dominant culture's code of race is based on a priori prejudice, and really prejudges individuals on the arbitrary basis of the mass status of the entire group. Although it does make occasional exceptions, more often it forces the advancing segments of the group back to the level and limitations of the less advanced.

Instead of gradually liquidating prejudice after emancipation, the behavior of members of the dominant culture, based on the rigid Anglo-Saxon tradition, tended to intensify racial tensions as the majority faced the ever-increasing challenges of the African American. Yet, in spite of this compounded discouragement and opposition, African Americans have shown epic achievement in all aspects of the dominant culture.

There exists a persistent disparity between the economic conditions of African Americans and those of members of the dominant culture that are a result of the racism of the past. Numerous civil rights laws, affirmative action regulations, and other public policies have not been able to remove these unequal conditions; indeed, in some areas they are becoming worse. Inequality in income, educational and occupational patterns, unemployment, and housing is influenced to a great extent by institutional racism; these areas show minor changes, if any.

Inequality in educational opportunity, performance, achievement, and outcomes is one major area where racial differences are apparent. School funding, quality, and completion rates at all levels are significant variables to note when studying racial differences. High school educational attainment among African Americans rose from 9.9 median years of school completed in 1970 to 12.0 in 1980. Of those African Americans 25 years old or older in 1980, only 51% had graduated from high school, while 70% of whites in the same age group held high school diplomas. In 1970, the dropout rate for 18 to 21-year-old African Americans was 30.5% and had decreased to 23% by 1980 (U.S. Department of Commerce, Bureau of the Census, 1981).

Despite these encouraging signs, there are still areas of concern that must be addressed. While the dropout rate is decreasing, in 1980 16% of African-American 14 to 24-year-olds had dropped out of school (U.S. Department of Commerce, Bureau of the Census, 1981). While it is important to keep students in school, it is even more important for them to graduate from school with skills or abilities that will make them useful citizens. Far too many youngsters leave school functionally illiterate, lacking the basic skills of reading, writing, and computation. As a result, they are relegated to low-paying, undesirable jobs.

The outlook for major changes in these and other areas of importance to African Americans is extremely grim. Perhaps the single most important impediment to change is the extent to which racism has become institutionalized. African Americans have worked to achieve equality through legal means, and the dominant culture has refused to accept them as equals. African Americans are likely to view the racial situation in the United States with greater urgency than are members of the dominant culture. The likelihood of major progress in eliminating racism is remote.

Sociopolitical Factors

With rare exceptions, African Americans have played a minor role in the formal political life of the United States (holding elected or appointed positions in government). Historically, African Americans have been heavily concentrated in the South, where various techniques have been used to keep them from participating in the electoral process. African-American politics has reflected an extensive range of forms and strategies, such as electoral politics, civil rights organizations, civic organizations, and policy process (through the courts).

The Fifteenth Amendment to the U.S. Constitution, passed in 1870, was the first attempt at ensuring participation of African Americans in the electoral process. The Voting Rights Act of 1965, and its subsequent amendments, has helped to overcome the disenfranchisement of millions of potential African-American voters. The Voting Rights Act was an attempt by Congress to enforce the Fifteenth Amendment. It mandated direct federal action that allowed African Americans to register and vote without having to rely upon litigation (U.S. Civil Rights Commission, 1968).

The success of the civil rights movement changed politics in the United States. In 1968, the first African-American candidates ran in a mayoral election against the established political machine. C. Young (1986) summarizes the mood and focus of the dominant culture:

> The general approach of the government to policy issues concerned with Afro-American affairs has been at best one of benign neglect. Disregard for the economic, social, political, and psychological well-being of black citizens is apparent in the deterioration of services, resources, and quality of life available to inner city residents. (p. 71)

Child-Rearing Practices

The role of African-American fathers has been explored within the context of the contemporary sociopolitical environment of all African Americans. In a study of child socialization patterns, Allen (1981) found that the child-rearing patterns of African-American parents reflect the reality that their sons are being socialized to be confrontive. He concludes that African-American parents recognize that future success for their sons hinges on an ability to be alternately and selectively assertive and acquiescent. According to Allen, the African-American mother's central role in her sons' lives is concerned with their interpersonal relations and their social life, while the father serves as a supporter in these areas.

Willie (1976) has described the environment of African-American children as not only including the special stresses of poverty and discrimination, but as an ambiguous and marginal one in which they live simultaneously in two worlds—the African-American world and the world of the dominant culture.

V. Young (1970) notes that the strict, no-nonsense discipline used by African-American parents, often characterized as harsh or rigid, is actually functional and appropriate discipline by caring parents. An inescapable aspect of the socialization of African-American children is that it prepares them for survival in an environment that is covertly, if not overtly, hostile, racist, and discriminatory against them.

Religious Practices

Religion has traditionally played an important role in the life of African Americans. The character of their religion is a reflection of their precarious status in the dominant culture. Denied the opportunity to participate as equals in the religious life and other institutions of the dominant culture, African Americans organized their own religious denominations as a means of coping with the social isolation they encountered.

African-American religious practices are an outgrowth of a complex historical process. The cultural traditions of West Africa were preserved directly in the lives of the slave population in the United States. Jules-Rosette (1980, p. 275) has identified six distinctive features of African spirituality that survived and became incorporated into the religious practices of African Americans:

(1) the direct link between the natural and supernatural

(2) the importance of human intervention in the supernatural world through possession and spiritual control

(3) the significance of music to invoke the supernatural

(4) the strong tie between the world of the living and the world of the dead in defining the scope of community

(5) the importance of participatory verbal performance, including the call-response pattern

(6) the primacy of both sacred and secular verbal performance

The central focus of African-American religion has been its ability to interpret the African-American experience in a meaningful way. The chief function of the African-American preacher has been and remains to make the Bible relevant to current events. As Henry (1990) states: "Black preaching is based on the Bible but not tied to pat legalistic or literalistic answers. Black worshipers are seeking the strength and assurance to survive another day rather than solutions to abstract theological problems" (p. 65).

With the emphasis on civil rights in the twentieth century, the African-American church has taken on a major role in advocating social change.

African-American ministers have become leaders in the civil rights movement, and the movement has continued to have a religious base. Henry (1990) characterizes the role of religion thus: "Black theology condemns capitalism, does not condemn violence, contends that God is actively working for black liberation, and demands reparations for past injustices" (p. 66).

African-American churches have always been more than religious institutions. During slavery, churches were centers for the development of leadership, educational institutions, and agents for the transmission of traditions and values of the African-American community. After emancipation, the functions of the churches increased as they became agents for strengthened family ties, employment agencies providing assistance to newcomers in locating housing and jobs, and cultural centers providing opportunities for African Americans to learn about and appreciate their own heritage.

The majority of African-American Christians are affiliated with the Baptist and Methodist denominations. The largest segments of these denominations are as follows: the National Baptist Convention U.S.A., 6.8 million members; the National Baptist Convention of America, 3.5 million members; the Progressive National Baptist Convention, 1.1 million members; and the African Methodist Episcopal Church, the African Methodist Episcopal Zion Church, the Christian Methodist Episcopal Church, and the United Methodist Church, which have a combined membership of approximately 6 million (Blackwell, 1985).

Family Structure and Dynamics

Franklin (1988) posits that the family is one of the strongest and most important traditions in the African-American community. Hill (1972) identifies five strengths of the African-American family: strong kinship bonds, strong work orientation, flexibility of family roles, strong achievement orientation, and strong religious orientation. He argues that these factors, which are not unique to African-American families, have been functional for the survival, advancement, and stability of African-American families. These strengths have been found in African-American communities in the form of informal day-care services, informal foster care, services to unwed mothers, and services to the elderly.

Asante (1981) has identified four aspects of Afrocentric male-female relationships that are based on teachings that man and woman are equally the source of strength and genius of African Americans. These four aspects are sacrifice, inspiration, vision, and victory. These elements provide the source and inspiration for all that men and women do together.

Staples (1981) provides insight on how external forces affect the internal stresses and strains that accompany the process of living in families. He challenges the myth of the African-American matriarchy, a myth that still exists to a great extent, in spite of numerous studies that have cast doubt on it. He concludes:

It has been functional for the white ruling class, through its ideological apparatus, to create internal antagonisms in the Black community between Black men and Black women to divide them and to ward off attacks on the external system of white racism. It is a mere manifestation of the divide-and-conquer strategy, used by most ruling classes through the annals of man, to continue the exploitation of an oppressed group. (p. 33)

No discussion of African-American family structure would be complete without some attention to the extended family. It is important to note that relationships with significant others, outside blood relatives, are essential to the maintenance of the family. In a study of extended families among African Americans, Manns (1981) found that significant others influenced the family in the following areas: modeling, validation of self, emotional support, achievement, socialization, and learning.

In addition to the extended family, Pinderhughes (1982) points out, the struggle to create a family system that can withstand the stress of the victim system has spawned a variety of family forms other than the traditional nuclear family. This is evident in the fact that in the African-American community the meaning of the term *parents* includes natural parents and grandparents as well as others who, at different times, assume parental roles and responsibilities.

Cultural Values and Attitudes

A number of distinctive characteristics of African-American cultural traits give strong credibility to the uniqueness of an African-American culture. Many of the characteristics of African-American culture are not found in the dominant culture. There is a connection between the cultural traits of African-American and other Afrocentric communities, such as the Caribbean. Finally, many of the elements of African-American culture are quite similar to elements found in West Africa, the location from which most of the slaves came.

Herskovits (1958) and Woodson (1968) have identified a number of cultural elements that are carryovers from Africa that have survived in the United States. These include dialect, folklore, adult-child relationships, family structure, music, generosity or hospitality, respect for the law, religion, sense of justice, and the work ethic.

One specific cultural value is that Africans have a different concept of time from that found in cultures of the Western world. This difference exists because Africans have no way of expressing a distant future. Another difference is that in traditional African societies, people emphasize whether something is done only at the present moment or done habitually. The Western view of time is linear, with an emphasis on what point on the time line an event occurs, that is, whether it is past, present, or future.

In becoming African Americans, the Africans had to develop a new framework capable of holding their beliefs, values, and behavior. What was useful from Africa was retained, what was useless was discarded, and new forms evolved from the old. This adaptive strategy allowed African Americans to carve out a world where they could get on with the business of living, building families and kinship groups, and a way of life capable of sustaining them under the conditions they found in the United States. African-American culture is testimony to the process of adaptation and cultural exchange (Turner & Perkins, 1976). While the cultures of West Africa differ in many ways, the traditional worldviews within them are remarkably similar. Among other things, each culture places a great deal of importance on family and kinship relationships, religion, and the care of children.

Hilliard (1976, pp. 38-39) describes the core cultural characteristics of African Americans as follows:

(1) They tend to respond to things in terms of the whole picture instead of its parts. The Euro-American tends to believe that anything can be divided and subdivided into pieces and that these pieces add up to a whole. Therefore, art is sometimes taught by numbers, as are dancing and music.

(2) They tend to prefer inferential reasoning to deductive or inductive reasoning.

(3) They tend to approximate space, numbers, and time rather than stick to accuracy.

(4) They tend to prefer to focus on people and their activities rather than on things. This tendency can be seen in the fact that so many African-American students choose careers in the helping professions, such as teaching, psychology, and social work.

(5) They tend to have a keen sense of justice and are quick to analyze and perceive injustice.

(6) They tend to lean toward altruism, a concern for fellow human beings.

(7) They tend to prefer novelty, freedom, and personal distinctiveness. This is shown in the development of improvisations in music and styles of clothing.

(8) They tend not to be "word" dependent. They tend to be very proficient in nonverbal communications.

A cultural nation is formed by a people with a common past, a common present, and, one hopes, a common future. The society may be that of the United States, but the values are African American. African-American values come only through an African-American culture. Culture is stressed because it gives identity, purpose, and direction. It tells you who you are, what you must do, and how you can do it. Without a culture, African-American values are only a set of reactions to the dominant culture. African-American culture is an expression of the desire of African Americans to decide their own destiny through control of their own political organizations and the establishment and preservation of their cultural, economic, and social institutions.

Implications

African-American children must be taught and must believe that deviations from the normative patterns of the dominant culture—such as Standard English—are not indications that they are abnormal. They must be helped to understand that negative social and psychological views have resulted in images of low self-esteem, identity crisis, and self-hatred. An appreciation of African-American cultural values is essential for African-American children if they are to develop positive self-identities. Despite the dominant culture's representations of deficiency or abnormality, a great many strengths serve as the foundation of African-American culture. Educators and counselors can work more effectively with African Americans if they begin from their students' or clients' points of strength. The strengths of the African-American family (Hill, 1972) and the core African-American cultural characteristics (Hilliard, 1976) should serve as background for any specific strategies developed for use with individuals or groups. Individuals from the dominant culture should not use themselves as sole reference points for how African-American children should behave. An individual's family and community, and how the person measures up to his or her peers, should provide additional reference points. In other words, African-American children's interactions with the dominant culture should be filtered through an African-American frame of reference.

Questions for Review and Reflection

(1) What event do you think has had the greatest influence on African Americans? Why?

(2) What are the ethnic group labels that have been associated with people of color whose roots are in Africa? What is the value associated with being called "African American"?

(3) Most African Americans are descendants of individuals who came to the United States as slaves, whereas individuals in most other ethnic groups in the United States are descendants of people who came to this country voluntarily. What influences has this difference had in terms of cultural identification? In terms of other factors?

(4) Why has the African-American church had so much influence on African-American culture?

(5) How does Black English influence the education of African Americans? Should African Americans be forced to abandon Black English? Why or why not?

(6) Which African-American cultural trait has influenced the education or counseling of African Americans the most? How?

(7) Discuss E. U. Essien-Udoms's (1962) concept of the "dilemma of duality."

(8) How would you describe the rank order of discrimination now in comparison to the rank order found by Myrdal in 1944? How does the ranking today influence educational or counseling practices?

(9) W. R. Allen (1981) has concluded that African-American fathers socialize their sons to be confrontive. How can educators or counselors use this knowledge in working with African-American males?

(10) How can educators or counselors use the cultural values reported by Hilliard (1976) in devising strategies and techniques for their work with African Americans?

References

Allen, W. R. (1981). Moms, dads and boys: Race and sex differences in the socialization of male children. In L. E. Gary (Ed.), *Black men* (pp. 99-114). Beverly Hills, CA: Sage.

Asante, M. (1981). Black male and female relationships: An Afrocentric context. In L. E. Gary (Ed.), *Black men* (pp. 75-82). Beverly Hills, CA: Sage.

Baratz, J. C. (1969). *Language and cognitive assessment of Negro children: Assumptions and research needs.* Washington, DC: Center for Applied Linguistics.

Billingsley, A. (1968). *Black families in white America.* Englewood Cliffs, NJ: Prentice-Hall.

Blackwell, J. E. (1985). *The Black community: Diversity and unity.* New York: Harper & Row.

Deutsch, M. (1965). The role of social class in language development and cognition. *American Journal of Orthopsychiatry, 35,* 78-88.

Dovidio, J. F., & Gaertner, S. L. (1986). *Prejudice, discrimination, and racism.* Orlando, FL: Academic Press.

Du Bois, W. E. B. (1961). *The souls of black folk: Essays and sketches.* New York: Fawcett. (Original work published 1910)

Essien-Udoms, E. U. (1962). *Black nationalism: A search for an identity in America.* Chicago: University of Chicago Press.

Franklin, J. H. (1988). A historical note on Black families. In H. P. McAdoo (Ed.), *Black families* (2nd ed., pp. 23-26). Newbury Park, CA: Sage.

Hale-Benson, J. E. (1982). *Black children: Their roots, culture, and learning styles.* Baltimore: Johns Hopkins University Press.

Henry, C. P. (1990). *Culture and African American politics.* Bloomington: Indiana University Press.

Herskovits, M. J. (1958). *The myth of the Negro past.* Boston: Beacon.

Hill, R. B. (1972). *The strengths of Black families.* New York: Emerson-Hall.

Hilliard, A. (1976). *Alternatives to IQ testing: An approach to the identification of gifted minority children* (Final report to the California State Department of Education). Sacramento: California State Department of Education.

Jules-Rosette, B. (1980). Creative spirituality from Africa to America: Cross-cultural influences in contemporary religious forms. *Western Journal of Black Studies, 4,* 273-285.

Malveaux, J. (1988). The economic statuses of Black families. In H. P. McAdoo (Ed.), *Black families* (2nd ed., pp. 133-147). Newbury Park, CA: Sage.

Manns, W. (1981). Support systems of significant others in Black families. In H. P. McAdoo (Ed.), *Black families* (pp. 238-251). Beverly Hills, CA: Sage.

Myrdal, G. (1944). *An American dilemma.* New York: Harper & Row.

Pinderhughes, E. B. (1982). Family functioning of Afro-Americans. *Social Work, 27,* 91-96.

Pinderhughes, E. B. (1989). *Understanding race, ethnicity, and power.* New York: Free Press.

Smitherman, G. (1977). *Talkin' and testifyin': The language of Black America.* Boston: Houghton Mifflin.

Staples, R. (1976). *Introduction to Black sociology.* New York: McGraw-Hill.

Staples, R. (1981). The myth of the Black matriarchy. *Black Scholar, 12,* 26-34.

Swinton, D. H. (1983). The economic status of the Black population. In National Urban League, *The state of Black America* (pp. 45-114). New York: National Urban League.

Turner, J., & Perkins, W. E. (1976). Slavery and Afro-American culture: Review essay. *Journal of Ethnic Studies, 3,* 80-87.

U.S. Civil Rights Commission. (1968). *Political participation.* Washington, DC: Government Printing Office.

U.S. Department of Commerce, Bureau of the Census. (1980). *1980 Census of the United States.* Washington, DC: Government Printing Office.

U.S. Department of Commerce, Bureau of the Census. (1981). *Statistical abstract of the United States.* Washington, DC: Government Printing Office.

Valentine, C. (1971). Deficit, difference, and bicultural models of Afro-American behavior. *Harvard Educational Review, 41,* 137-157.

Willie, C. V. (1976). *A new look at Black families.* New Bayside, NY: General Hall.

Woodson, C. G. (1968). *The African background outlined.* New York: Negro Universities Press.

Young, C. (1986). Afro-American family: Contemporary issues and implications for social policy. In D. Pilgrim (Ed.), *On being Black: An in-group analysis* (pp. 58-75). Bristol, IN: Wyndham Hall.

Young, V. (1970). Family and childhood in a southern Negro community. *American Anthropologist, 72,* 269-288.

3

Amish

Old Order Amish culture has changed little in 300 years. It varies in only minor ways in districts across the United States, despite the absence of telephones and the limits of horse-and-buggy travel. The agrarian life-style of the Amish is defined by simplicity, hard work, integrity, order, and community.

Followers of Mennonite elder Jacob Amman broke from the Mennonite church in Germany to form the Amish sect in the late 1600s. The first Amish settled in the United States around 1737 (Wittmer, 1990). The Amish, Mennonites, and Moravians settled at William Penn's invitation in his colony. Many European Amish gradually assimilated into other religions and no longer exist separately. Although the Amish have never been averse to relocating, the largest Amish settlements in the United States remain in Lancaster County, Pennsylvania. To the west, Holmes County, Ohio, and Buchanan County, Iowa, are also home to large Amish communities (Hudson, 1981).

Old Order Amish, the most conservative and traditional, are also known as House Amish, because they hold services in private homes. They are distinguished from the New, Church, and Beachy Amish, who do not thoroughly accept modern American culture, but have fewer qualms about using labor-saving technology and associating with "English," their term for non-Amish (Hostetler, 1980). They are also distinguished from Mennonites, Moravians, and Black Car Amish.

Acculturation

Old Order Amish culture is based on two verses of scripture: "Be not conformed to this world: but be ye transformed by the renewing of your mind, that ye may prove what is that good, and acceptable, and perfect, will of God" (Romans 12:2), and "Be ye not unequally yoked together with unbelievers; for what fellowship hath righteousness with unrighteousness? And what communion hath light with darkness?" (II Corinthians 6:14). Accordingly, Amish seek as complete a separation from the world as possible.

The Amish do many things to maintain their culture and identity. Some of these practices, values, and beliefs include the exclusion of the outside world for all things except the purchase of essential necessities; the observance of strict rules of behavior, dress, language usage, education, and religion; a sequential socialization process; the strong involvement of the extended family; and a rich sense of community and mutual aid that is woven through the Amish way of life (Good, 1985). The Amish refusal to be acculturated has resulted in "hostility and harassment and it is becoming increasingly more difficult for the Amish to preserve their peace-loving values in America" (Wittmer, 1990, p. 6)

Poverty and Economic Concerns

Unlike most oppressed groups in the United States today, the Amish are not deprived of the ability to secure enough to eat and live in suitable quarters. However, to some outsiders, the Amish choice of a way of life may seem much like poverty. The Amish can live very cheaply by dressing plainly; by building or making most of their clothes, houses, and barns; by not using electricity; and by not owning any modern conveniences or machines. If anyone in the community is in need, everyone comes to that person's assistance. Their simple way of life, coupled with a tradition of community aid, has enabled the Amish to be both healthy and prosperous.

History of Oppression

Oppression of the Amish has its origins in the social, economic, and religious upheavals experienced in Europe as far back as the sixteenth century. The Amish are direct descendants of the Anabaptist movement in Switzerland. The Anabaptists, which literally means "rebaptizer," were severely persecuted by the Roman church and the reformers, such as the Lutherans, because they represented a "third" option: a belief that Christians are adults who voluntarily confess their faith and subsequently are baptized, as in the early Christian church.

The torment faced by the Anabaptists in Europe was implemented by secret police called "Anabaptist hunters" who were trained to spy on the Anabaptists and finally arrest them. Their fate was then imprisonment or banishment, coupled with confiscation of property (which was ultimately sold to defray the costs of the spies), and imprisonment. Special rewards were given to any hunter who captured an Anabaptist leader.

The children of Anabaptists were deemed illegitimate because their parents had not been married by reformed ministers, and therefore they could not inherit their parents' estates. Because of the Anabaptists' refusal to baptize infants, serve in the military, or take oaths, even in the face of imprisonment, they were often sold as galley slaves. Often, Anabaptist men were taken to the border, branded with hot irons, and then forced into exile.

The Amish history of persecution forced them to develop dependence on the mutual assistance of their own, gave them a reluctance to change, and created distrust of those outside their group. It was due in part to their reluctance to change that the Amish, led by Jacob Amman, split from the Mennonites in the late seventeenth century over the use of *Meidung* (shunning of the excommunicated). The Amish believed in this practice, and the Mennonites did not. The Amish have also suffered many other divisions since their beginnings.

Ironically, the Amish migrated to the New World to escape religious persecution, both during the first half of the 1700s and between 1815 and 1860. However, even in the United States they encountered problems because they would not take an oath of allegiance or join the military. During the Revolutionary War the Amish were viewed as patriots aligned with the British. They were not allowed to serve on juries, to sue within the law, to hold public office, or to buy or sell land. Some Amish were charged with treason and were held in jail.

This oppression served to galvanize the Amish, who stressed "man's duty to glorify God by full and unyielding obedience." They risked coming to the New World to "make a beginning free from the restraints to which they were subjected back home" (Hudson, 1981). The Amish struggle for freedom to exercise their beliefs continues in the twentieth century, as the Old Order Amish are pitted against the U.S. government in matters concerning educational freedom and the freedom to live apart from society and apart from the advances of technology.

Language and the Arts

The Amish create little art for art's sake. Their art is manifest in the simplicity and symmetry of their gardens, solid furnishings, and hand-fashioned household items. They do not create art by writing poetry or novels, or by painting or drawing. Although *art* is probably not a term the Amish would use to describe their work skills, Amish art is found in the crafts and vocational skills that the Amish possess and use.

SCHOOL'S OUT
James Ashbrook Perkins

Caught forever
In the moment
Of his joy
Not by a camera
Which he would avoid
But by my eye
An Amish boy
His hat flung
Wild before him
Exploding out the door
Of his one-room school
To land barefoot
On the warming earth
Eager
To get to his father's field
And begin
His summer's education.

James Ashbrook Perkins, author of this poem, is not Amish; the poem is part of a collection of poems and woodcuts by two professors at Westminster College in Pennsylvania (Oestreich & Perkins, 1976). This is an "outsider's" artistic view of the Amish world expressed in poetry. As suggested by the poem, most Amish people receive a formal education only up to the eighth-grade level. Formal education is valued far less among the Amish than is the education one gains through experience and hard work on the farm.

Most Amish are farmers by trade, but all participate in the one-day craft of barn raising. By bringing an entire community together for one day for the sole purpose of building a barn, the task is completed with incredible artful skill. This form of mutual aid also extends to other Amish "art forms," such as the beautiful quilts that are made by the women. In general, the "arts" of the Amish are utilitarian products that are completed by groups of people and not by individuals.

An Amish home may be decorated with a calendar or a photograph of the farm, but no pictures of people are used. The Amish do not allow themselves to be photographed. Colorful braided rugs may cover the floors, especially in winter, for insulation. Quilts, many completed in the same dark colors as

Amish clothing, with the addition of white backgrounds, are made for use, not display. Friendship quilts are popular. Each woman in a group creates an original square, often sewing in the names of family members. The group then meets to assemble and quilt the finished product and to present it as a gift. The same process is used to produce quilts for sale (Hostetler & Huntington, 1971).

Just as Amish art is utilitarian in nature, the languages spoken by the Amish have specific uses and purposes. The Amish speak three distinct tongues: Pennsylvania German, High German, and English. Their native Pennsylvania German is the primary oral language; they have a passing command of High German for reading the Bible or quoting it aloud with their own distinctive pronunciation; and they can read, write, and speak English without interference of their other languages.

Pennsylvania German, or "Pennsylvania Dutch," as it is sometimes called, is the preferred spoken language and is used exclusively in the home and the community. It is the mother tongue of children born to Amish parents. The Amish High German, or "the language of the Bible," is used exclusively for the preaching service and on formal ceremonial occasions. An Amish person does not converse in High German. The children are taught how to read High German in school, but many do not fully understand its meaning.

English is learned out of necessity. It is the responsibility of the school-teacher to teach English. English is spoken all the time at school, except for designated High German classes, or perhaps on the playground, where the children might speak Pennsylvania Dutch. English is considered the language of the world. There is currently some fear in the Amish community that English is being preferred by the children over the traditional Pennsylvania Dutch.

Four current Amish publications can provide additional information for those interested in the most contemporary information about the Amish. The *Budget* is a weekly newspaper published in Sugarcreek, Ohio, by non-Amish for the Amish. This newspaper uses a reporter from each Amish community who writes a weekly column with information on births, illnesses, deaths, and the like. There are no comics and no editorials. The other three publications, *Young Companion, Family Life,* and *Blackboard Bulletin,* are published by Pathway Publishers, whose writers and publishers are Old Order Amish. They use innovative nonmodern methods to produce these publications (Wittmer, 1990).

Racism and Prejudice

Since the founding of the Amish way of life, religious, social, and legal persecution has limited the group's freedom. During the seventeenth century, the Amish were hunted, sold as slaves, and stripped of their dignity as a result of differences in their religious beliefs compared with those of the dominant churches.

After migrating to the United States in hopes of living in a freer environment, the Amish were met with skepticism when they refused to fight for "their country." They were treated as traitors by people who could not understand their pacifist position.

As a result of their distinctive customs, many people deride them for being different. They are often referred to as "backward" or "ignorant." The popular movie *Witness* included a scene, based in reality, in which a group of outsiders hit and spat upon a group of Amish men, taking advantage of their nonviolent stance. Some of these negative attitudes have translated into tragedy. In one case, an Amish baby in Indiana was killed by an object thrown into the family's buggy by scornful neighborhood youths passing by in a speeding truck (Hostetler & Huntington, 1971).

Like other minorities, the Amish endure verbal affronts as well. In Buchanan County they are often pejoratively called "hookies," a term that refers to the Amish use of hooks and eyes instead of buttons.

The laws have also made it difficult for the Amish to practice their religious beliefs fully. For many years, one of the major issues threatening the Amish culture was compulsory school attendance. Following a long struggle and a Supreme Court decision, however, an exemption clause was written for the Amish, exempting them from compulsory high school attendance. Another legal issue that created a problem for the Amish was that of compulsory social security payments. The Amish believe in taking no aid from the government, thus the law that forced them to pay social security taxes violated their beliefs. The Amish were eventually excluded from mandatory payments.

Sociopolitical Factors

Despite their separatist tendencies, the Amish interact with the outside world in a continuum spanning from global generosity to governmental confrontation via passive resistance. On the one side of the issue, the Amish strongly support local charities and specific worldwide relief organizations. On the opposite side, the Amish have been forced into numerous legal battles that have threatened the open practice of their religious beliefs and ideals. Since the Amish are "defenseless Christians," they will not defend themselves in court. Their cases are usually argued by the National Committee for Amish Religious Freedom, a non-Amish group. The Amish people's resistance to change, or rather their steadfastness in their beliefs, has compelled the courts to consider landmark decisions supporting freedom for the Amish to practice those beliefs.

The Amish are active in supporting local charities that aid the general welfare of the community, such as fire and emergency services. Benefit auctions for specific needs, such as a new ambulance, are attended by and heavily supported by the Amish. Organizations for the blind and the handicapped are often supported by the Amish. Many of the Amish support their Mennonite cousins in two worldwide relief organizations. They participate in global assistance through the Mennonite Central Committee (MCC), which distributes millions of dollars of aid and service to many countries in the name of Christ. Quilts, crafts, and food are sold at public relief sales to benefit the MCC and a second relief organization called the Mennonite Disaster Service. When major disasters strike, groups of Amish volunteer their time to work in the ruined areas throughout North America (Good, 1985).

Although generous in supporting the general welfare of all people throughout the world, the Amish hold a less open position toward the U.S. government, perhaps due in part to their ancestral persecution by governments in Europe and by the U.S. government as well. The Amish are respectful of local, state, and federal governments, but they are also wary. Like their forefathers, the Amish acknowledge the need for government to maintain order in the "carnal" world; however, the authority of the state is not applicable to the spiritual realm.

Given this belief, the Amish do not run for public office, and they do not resort to courts of law to settle disputes among themselves or with outsiders. They cannot take oaths, serve on juries, or collect debts by using the courts. The Amish do pay their taxes, except for the social security tax exemption that was granted under the Johnson administration in 1965. Crime rates in general tend to be low in Amish communities. The Amish tend to be involved as little as possible in the political machine in the United States (Warner & Denlinger, 1969).

Nonetheless, many of the firm beliefs of the Amish have been analyzed and questioned by the courts. Nearly 300 years after the first Amish settlers came to the New World to escape religious persecution, the Amish still are threatened by the dominant culture in exercising their constitutional freedoms. Some examples of the government analysis of their rights include the Iowa school incident, the compulsory education issue, and the compulsory welfare problem.

The Iowa school incident, which took place during the mid-1960s, involved conflict between Buchanan County officials and the Amish community. In short, the community was forced to send the Amish children to nearby "adequate" schools because the two Amish schools did not have "appropriately certified teachers," did not teach "adequate curriculum," and did not provide "proper facilities." After many conflicts, the Amish were allowed to keep their schools intact through a special grant from a private foundation that paid for the certified staff. Some saw this as an overwhelming victory for the Amish (Keim, 1975).

Another education issue the Amish have had to deal with is that of compulsory education. Many in the Amish community perceive compulsory education as a threat and obstacle to the Amish way of life. In the past, some states required school attendance of all children until they were 16 years old. After imprisonment of Amish fathers unwilling to pay fines or to comply with the compulsory education law, feeling that it violated their religious beliefs, the landmark case of *Wisconsin v. Yoder* was heard by the U.S. Supreme Court. The Court ruled that "enforcement of the State's requirement of compulsory formal education after the eighth grade would gravely endanger if not destroy the free exercise of . . . [Amish] religious beliefs" (Keim, 1975).

As mentioned above, another law that compelled the Amish to violate their beliefs was the compulsory welfare law. The Amish are opposed to any dependency on government; rather, they support the principal of self-sufficiency in caring for the elderly, widows, and orphans. They refuse any type of government assistance. In 1955, when social security benefits were extended to cover self-employed persons, including farmers, the Amish were required to make payments in the form of social security taxes. However, after much resistance, an exemption clause was granted to the Amish that excludes them from compulsory welfare payments.

In summary, the relationship between the Amish community and the outside world has been one of mixed exchanges. Although generous in giving to those in need, whatever their political identifications, the Amish continue to resist any changes created by technology and the so-called upgrading of American society. They remain passive but determined and firm in their convictions.

Child-Rearing Practices

Unlike most of mainstream America, the Amish are child centered in their structuring of everyday life. Some would argue that Amish children are forced to lead restricted lives that stifle their individualism; however, there are many positive aspects to Amish child-rearing practices. Amish children are content and surrounded by security, there are clear expectations and structures for them, and they have numerous role models both inside and outside their extended families, as well as a sense of community belonging. Both parents are intimately involved in the socialization of the children as teachers, role models, and consistent disciplinarians.

Parents are an integral part of their children's development at each of the four recognized stages: infancy, preschool, scholars, and young people. Each stage corresponds with specific responsibilities to accept and specific tasks to learn. The first stage covers the period from birth until the child walks; children in this stage are called "babies." The second stage spans the period between walking and entrance to school, which is usually age 6 or 7; preschool children are sometimes called "little children." Children attending school are called "scholars," and they fulfill the eighth-grade minimum requirement for school attendance. After schooling is complete, the children are called "youth" or "young people" and are required to complete a regular adult day's work. Baptism signifies religious adulthood, and marriage and the birth of the first child signify social adulthood (Hostetler & Huntington, 1971).

Babies are considered special gifts from God and not primarily extensions of the parents. A baby is considered blameless and can do no wrong. There is no such thing as a bad baby, although there may be a difficult one. If the baby cries, he or she is comforted, not disciplined. Within the security of the home, babies are lovingly handled by persons of all ages and are rarely alone. They are rarely fed on a strict schedule; rather, they are fed when they are hungry. The openness and affection displayed toward babies within the community contrasts with the way babies are exposed to the outside world. When a mother goes outside the community, she wraps her baby up tightly and carries him or her under her shawl.

During the preschool years the "little children," as they are called, learn to respect and obey those in authority, to care for those younger and less able, to share with others and help others, to do what is right and avoid what is wrong, and to complete work responsibilities pleasantly. Obedience is based on love and respect; the child learns that the adult authority has his or her best interests always in mind. Blind obedience is not encouraged. However, there are consistent consequences for disobedience, defiance, or stubbornness. A switch may be used, but not harshly (Hostetler & Huntington, 1971).

Work is viewed as a collective helping of others, and independence is discouraged. Little children are expected to complete certain tasks, such as running errands around the farm, and are never thanked for carrying out these responsibilities. Boys and girls at this age do similar tasks. Finally, at this stage, the asking of "why" questions is stifled; children are encouraged to observe and imitate behavior, not to ask intellectual questions.

At the scholar stage, children between the ages of 6 and 15 continue to be reinforced with the cultural values of the Amish community by their parents. Scholars are motivated not by fear of punishment, but by concern for other people. Although children at this age attend Amish schools or public schools, the main responsibility for religious and social training lies with the parents. Parents fear that children will become indoctrinated by outside ideas, and thus the unity of faith, family, and community would be broken.

Despite parental fears, laws require Amish children to attend school at least until the eighth grade. Before the 1930s, all Amish children attended public schools, but in recent decades Amish communities have maintained their own schools. Most Amish schools have one room and one teacher for all eight grades. Younger children learn by listening to older children recite their lessons. The schools teach the "three Rs"—reading, writing, and arithmetic—and they meet state standards concerning the number and length of school days.

After completion of the eighth grade, the young people are discouraged from going on to high school because this is considered unnecessary and worldly. Instead, the boys are taught the essentials of farming and the girls are taught the basics of homemaking. Often the young people will test the limits of their community by engaging in "non-Amish" activities such as owning a radio or wearing non-Amish clothing. The young people are not forced to join the Amish religion; a child may make a decision to be baptized, and thus enter religious adulthood. Marriage usually does not occur until young people are in their 20s.

During all their stages of development—as babies, little children, scholars, and young people—Amish children are influenced by the consistent and compassionate care of their parents. Although seemingly rigid in methods, Amish parents do allow their children to make the major decision of religious and social inclusion; of course, the consequence of not choosing the Amish way is lifelong shunning from the community.

Religious Practices

The Amish are primarily users of the New Testament. The Dordrecht Confession of Faith, written in Holland in 1632, is the basis of the *Ordnung,* district rules and standards. A sense of community and togetherness permeates the religious practices of the Amish people. For them, the sacred power is found within the community, and not outside of it. The Amish have no religious scholars who interpret the Bible; rather, each person models the teachings of the sacred book without debating its content. The Bible is to be used ritualistically, never didactically or intellectually. Some of the Amish rituals include the preaching service, communion, foot washing, and baptism (Schwieder & Schwieder, 1975).

The all-day preaching service is held every other week at the homes of various members of the church on a rotating basis. There is much preparation required in the hosting of the service, from preparing the house and the stables to cooking the meal that is shared. Everyone attends the services, even infants. The formal part of the service may last up to three hours, including the singing of hymns a cappella (one hymn may take 20-30 minutes to sing), prayers, Bible readings, several sermons, testimonials, and community announcements. There is a set order by which people must enter and exit from the room, and special seating assignments are also used.

Communion, a ritual that is practiced twice a year, binds the Amish members together in mutual dependency. It also requires the Amish person to experience a personal examination two weeks prior to the communion service in order to prepare for the taking of communion. During the day-long communion service, children are kept in a separate place while the adults participate in the ritual. Communion includes the humble practice of washing one another's feet, as Jesus did at the Last Supper.

Finally, baptism is offered once a year to young people who have decided to join the Amish faith as spiritual adults. The Amish do not believe in infant baptism; this is one of the focal issues that separated the Amish from other religious groups.

Although the rituals of the Amish Christian faith are practiced with other community members, it is only the parents who teach their children about the Bible; adults never teach children other than their own about the Bible. Religion is not taught specifically at school. It is thought that since Christianity pervades all life, it will naturally emerge in all school subjects. It is believed that the Bible is taught by example, not by lecture. For example, the parents dress, behave, and make decisions according to the proper Christian way, to set an example for their children. The Amish do not proselytize. Their aim is to preserve rather than to promote their way of life (Hostetler & Huntington, 1971).

Some of the overt appearance and behavioral practices that the adults "model" include a pacifist stand on violence or the bearing of arms; refraining from worldly pleasurable activities such as dancing or attending card parties, theaters, or amusement parks; abstention from drinking liquor or smoking cigarettes; and the refusal to own radios, jewelry, phones, or other modern devices. Through parental example, the children learn the appropriate morals of the Amish culture.

Like all aspects of the Amish life, religious practices are structured, consistent, simple, and unchanging. The Amish favor close ties with the soil because of the biblical parables that connect people with nature and the land. The two most important lessons learned from nature and the soil are the main focus of the Amish religion. First, one learns that a seed, placed in the earth, must die before it can give birth. The images of death and resurrection surround the farmer. Second, one learns that one reaps what one sows, either in this life or in the next.

Family Structure and Dynamics

The family is the basic unit of Amish culture; it provides nurturing, stability, and socialization. One illustration of this is that the size of a church district is measured not by the number of baptized persons, but by the number of families or households in the district. An Amish schoolteacher will tell you how many families attend her school, and when she introduces the children, she will often introduce them by family rather than by grade. The Amish emphasize the group over the individual. The family has authority over the individual in childhood, adolescence, and beyond.

The main functions of the Amish family are procreation, nurture, and socialization of children. Families are monogamous in formation and patriarchal in authority. The family comes first. A job is of no intrinsic importance; it is necessary only to provide economic support for one's family. The activities of the community, such as church services, are centered around family units joining together.

The average Amish household has 7 children, but some have as many as 14. Married couples are expected to take on the responsibility of having and rearing children. Parents spend a large portion of their time teaching their children appropriate behaviors and useful skills in maintaining the Christian life.

In marriage, husband and wife become "one flesh," a union that can be terminated only in death. Divorce is not an option in the Amish community. In keeping with biblical law, the man is the head of the woman and the household, although the wife does have some voice. For example, in the church, although the woman must be silent for the most part, she does have an equal vote. A woman is also allowed to decide individually whether or not she is ready to take communion. She does follow her husband's decisions for the family, but there is often some mutual discussion before he makes the final decision. However, should her husband sin to the extent that he is placed under the ban, she, like all members of the community, will shun him. The husband would do the same if his wife were under the ban.

In practice, the farm is the Amish man's kingdom, and his wife is his general manager of household affairs. The man helps only nominally in household tasks. The wife's duties include care of the children, cooking and cleaning, preparation of food for market, making clothes for the family, preserving food, and gardening. Children assist with these tasks as they are able.

Marriage partners are to be considerate of each other and never disagree in public. Similarly, their personal relationship is quiet and reserved, and there is never any open display of affection. The expectation of romance popular in the mainstream American culture is not part of Amish culture; no terms of endearment or physical gestures are used. The marriage norm is not love, but respect.

As with all community activities, the extended family is involved in the socialization of and modeling for the children. Often grandparents, who may retire as early as 50, will assist in the care of the young children. The older people of the community are respected and are often consulted about questions regarding farming, cooking, building, and so on.

Retirement is gradual, unless children need farms. Older people are revered as keepers of knowledge and tradition, and may work or rest as they like, gradually taking more time for visiting and for avocations such as needlework, toy making, or raising flowers. As a son and his family take over the running of the farm, they also take over the house. The older couple may move to the "Grossdawdy's (grandfather's) House," a smaller house to the side of the main house (Wittmer, 1990). Older people remain active and useful. When the end comes, they are cared for and die at home (Hostetler & Huntington, 1971).

The family is the stabilizing structure in the Amish community. It is central to the activities of all community members' the daily lives. Only God comes before the family. The family bond spreads out to the community to form a unified, mutually nurturing group of people.

Cultural Values and Attitudes

The Amish people hold a unique set of cultural values and attitudes. Although living solely in the here and now, they are working toward the ultimate everlasting life in heaven with God. Children are born into the world without sin or evil; this is illustrated in the practice of adult baptism rather than infant baptism. They live in subjugation to God, following God's will as revealed in the Bible. An Amish person interacts with others in the community in a collateral way; everyone is part of the "family." This method of communication is not extended to the "outside" world.

Hostetler and Huntington (1971) identify five main values of the Old Order Amish. The first is separation from the world. The Amish view the world as containing opposites, such as good and evil, light and darkness. It is the duty of each person to keep him- or herself "unspotted from the world." This is accomplished in part by minimizing contact with the outside world; such contact is sanctioned only to secure essential necessities with which to live. An Amish person could never marry or become a business partner with a non-Amish person.

The Amish also set themselves apart from the world by not participating in any form of violence or war. They do not use any type of self-defense and will more readily move from an area than try to defend their rights. Their refusal to serve in the military has caused them considerable difficulty with the U.S. government, dating to the Revolutionary War.

Second, voluntary acceptance of high social obligations is symbolized by adult baptism. This is a very serious commitment, from which there is no turning back. Men vow at baptism to accept the call to minister, if they are chosen. Through voluntary adult baptism, the Amish person becomes a member of the Amish Christian faith, which has many social and moral obligations. Some of these include the responsibilities of raising children under the proper rules, contributing to the continuance of the society, and being a part of community activities such as barn raisings.

Maintenance of a disciplined church community is a third value. Few rules are in writing, and the *Ordnung* may vary with the district. Questionable issues must be resolved "with unanimous expression of peace and good will" (p. 6) twice a year before communion is offered. The religious symbolism of the Amish is conveyed in their dress and physical appearance. Their style of dress is a protest against the proud and disobedient world. An Amish man wears a full beard, simple black clothing with no outside or hip pockets or suspenders, and a black hat with a 3-inch brim. Women may not wear silk or showy garments; they must wear plain dresses that hang within 8 inches of the floor, and their hair must remain uncut, with no styling or curling. Women must also wear aprons, shawls, and bonnets of proper size and color at appropriate times.

Fourth, the practices of excommunication and shunning are strictly enforced. In an effort to keep the church pure, the Amish utilize excommunication (*Bann*) and shunning (*Meidung*) with members who break the rules of the faith. Members not "in fellowship" with the group, meaning not living according to the *Ordnung,* must be "expelled from the fellowship just as the human body casts off an infectious growth" (p. 7). Excommunication bans the person from sharing communion. Shunning involves the total avoidance of a person in social, economic, and religious realms. No member can eat at the same table with an excommunicated/shunned person. If the person under the ban is a husband or wife, the couple must suspend marital relations. Members may not exchange favors or services or have social or sexual interaction with shunned persons until they publicly repent.

Finally, life must be in harmony with soil and nature. Man is viewed as caretaker, not conqueror or exploiter, of nature. The austere life-style of the Amish ensures few expenses and few repairs. Each farm can be self-sufficient, raising vegetables, pigs, and dairy cows, and selling eggs, extra horses, honey, maple syrup, lumber, and handmade quilts. The Amish use steel wheels on their vehicles, which reduces possible farm size, since steel wheels cannot be run on public roads between fields (many Amish communities now permit a small strip of rubber on vehicle wheels). Small farms mean enough farms for all, which prevents affluence and a tenant class, especially important because affluent young work less, have more time to explore worldly ways, and are more likely to leave the church.

Like their pacifist, Anabaptist forefathers, the Amish will move rather than fight to protect their way of life. Mobility is a respected safety valve in the preservation of culture. When a district grows too large, when land prices increase beyond the means of young marrieds, when disagreement cannot be mediated, Amish communities separate and move apart in friendship.

Provided the differences are not too great, the groups maintain "kinship ties and visiting patterns."

The Future

Old Order districts are currently found in more than 20 states, with the largest concentrations in Illinois, Iowa, Kansas, Minnesota, Mississippi, Oklahoma, and Wisconsin, in addition to the extensive communities in Pennsylvania and Ohio. They have also migrated into Central and South America and Canada. As the dominant culture encroaches on and restricts their way of life, the Amish will no doubt continue to move as long as affordable farmland is available. Perhaps they will concentrate in Arkansas, where there are already one Beachy Amish and one Amish Mennonite community. Because of the modern irrigation and other practices required to farm on the Great Plains, it is unlikely they will go further west (Schwieder & Schwieder, 1975).

When the Amish came to the United States, their ways and outward appearance differed little from those of their neighbors. As the world grows increasingly complex, the Amish maintain their simple, self-sufficient ways, bringing differences into sharper focus. Despite the lure of the world, the Amish continue to hold on to a large majority of their youth. Schwieder and Schwieder (1975) estimate an Old Order Amish defection rate—that is, young people refusing to join the church—of 10-15%. Of that group, 95% stay "close to home," joining either Beachy Amish or Mennonite groups.

The Amish are resilient, compromising only when absolutely necessary to maintain their families and communities, and moving on when compromise is too threatening. As long as there is affordable land to farm, the Amish will compromise, relocate, and survive.

Questions for Review and Reflection

(1) What influence does the practice of limiting education to the eighth grade have on the Amish culture?

(2) What is "shunning"? How does this practice affect the psychological health of the shunned person?

(3) Which Amish cultural practice do you find most desirable for you as a member of your cultural group? Why?

(4) What Amish cultural traits appeal to you as desirable and potentially useful to the dominant culture? Why?

(5) What stereotypes do you hold relative to the Amish people? How might the stereotypes facilitate or hinder your work with Amish students or clients?

(6) What is the basis of Amish "separation from the world"?

(7) How do Amish art and language differ from those of the dominant culture?

(8) How do the stereotypes of "ignorant" and "backward" influence your view of Amish culture?

(9) What steps would you take to resolve a conflict between the Amish culture and laws in the dominant culture?

(10) What principles would guide your interactions with an Amish youth who desires to leave the Amish community?

References

Good, M. (1985). *Who are the Amish?* Intercourse, PA: Good Books.

Hostetler, J. A. (1980). *Amish society.* Baltimore: Johns Hopkins University Press.

Hostetler, J. A., & Huntington, G. E. (1971). *Children in Amish society: Socialization and community education.* New York: Holt.

Hudson, W. S. (1981). *Religion in America.* New York: Scribner's.

Keim, A. (1975). *Compulsory education and the Amish: The right not to be modern.* Boston: Beacon.

Oestreich, N., & Perkins, J. (1976). *The Amish: Two perceptions.* New Wilmington, PA: Dawn Valley.

Schwieder, E., & Schwieder, D. (1975). *A peculiar people: Iowa's Old Order Amish.* Ames: Iowa University Press.

Warner, J., & Denlinger, D. (1969). *A portrait of the Amish.* New York: Grossman.

Wittmer, J. (1990). *The gentle people: Personal reflections of Amish life.* Minneapolis: Educational Media Corporation.

4

Native Americans

One of the great tragedies of exploitation of culturally different groups in the United States has been the consistent and long-standing maltreatment of Native Americans. Motivated by self-interest and a quest for power over people and natural resources, white Europeans and their descendants invaded the territorial homelands of this country's aboriginal inhabitants well into the twentieth century. Forcibly pushed from their sacred and valuable lands, Native Americans throughout the Americas found themselves virtually stripped of their cultural identity and relegated to property unwanted by whites. In many respects, Native American culture has been approached superficially by historians and other researchers, whose writings have traditionally concentrated on the development and expansion of Anglocentric culture in the United States. The popular entertainment media have almost invariably distorted accurate views of American Indian culture. The result of these biases often has been misunderstanding by the general populace and a broad stereotyping of richly complex peoples.

Some ambiguity exists about the name that should be used for the population discussed in this chapter. Historically, the name *Indian* was used, followed by *American Indian* and, more recently, *Native American.* The Bureau of Indian Affairs (BIA) (1988) defines a Native American as one who is a registered or enrolled member of a tribe or whose blood quantum is one-fourth or more, genealogically derived. Hirschfelder (1982) reports that one

Native American law center has assembled 52 legal definitions of Native Americans. The U.S. Census Bureau, on the other hand, records anyone who claims native identity as Native American. Although there appears to be no consensus as to the most appropriate term, *Native American* is used here because it connotes both the heritage of the original inhabitants of this continent and the group's current status as U.S. citizens.

There have been a great many tribal groups of Native Americans living throughout the United States, and it is impossible to say that there is any one culture associated with all Native Americans per se. Native Americans constitute less than 1% of the population of the United States. This heterogeneous, geographically dispersed group speaks some 150 tribal languages in 505 federally recognized and 365 state-recognized tribal groups (Bureau of Indian Affairs, 1988). The majority of Native Americans live west of the Mississippi River, with 40% of the total population living in Arizona, California, New Mexico, Oklahoma, and Washington. More than half of the total Native American population resides in urban areas, and about one-fourth live on the 52 million acres of land identified as reservations (Stock, 1987). Even in the face of this vast diversity, however, "it can be said that it is possible to isolate unifying and consistent patterns of behavior among Indian individuals as well as among Indian tribes" (Washburn, 1975, p. xvi). And Thomason (1991) concludes that "there are some similarities in the basic values and beliefs of many Native Americans" (p. 326). It is on the premise that there are similarities among Native Americans that a composite view of this group's culture may be drawn. However, the existence of these similarities should not result in a conclusion that Native Americans are one group with one need. In fact, the material in this chapter emphasizes qualities/characteristics of reservation Native Americans, individuals quite different from nonreservation Native Americans.

Acculturation

A testimony to this fact is that, in spite of the assault by the overarching dominant American culture on Native American life, many Native Americans have not become acculturated. Opposition to acculturation shows dramatically how very different Native American perspectives on and assumptions about the world are from Eurocentric values and traditions. As Yates (1987) has stated:

> On the whole, American Indian tribes are remarkable in that they have withstood attempts at extermination, removal from their traditional lands, extreme poverty, deployment of their youth to boarding schools, relocation policies, and last but not least, the white man's poison—alcohol. (p. 1135)

Some Native Americans eagerly accepted and adopted such aspects of European culture as Christianity and clothing. Their being able to move back and forth between two cultures so readily is easily understood when one considers the Native Americans' holistic view of the universe, in which all things are seen as equally important (Sue & Sue, 1990). Among the Tuscaroras, for example, changes in customs and modifications in culture occurred quite frequently among the different Native American tribes because of their practice of assimilating after being captured in war (Johnson, 1967).

Despite the willingness of some Native Americans to become bicultural, the newcomers to their world were intent upon acculturating and/or terminating Native Americans almost from the beginning. This policy was and still is most easily seen in the American educational system. Thomas Jefferson espoused an educational system that would "educate men to manners, morals, and habits perfectly homogeneous with those of the country" (Foreman, 1987, p. 2). The "manners, morals, and habits" of which Jefferson spoke were those of native Englishmen, not those of Native Americans. This attempt to force the acculturation of Native Americans is still prevalent in our educational system today (Pertusati, 1988).

Poverty and Economic Concerns

The dominant culture of the United States has forced Native Americans to become intimate with the concept of poverty. According to O'Connell (1985), "Native Americans represent the most economically disadvantaged and underserved group in America. They have the lowest average income, lowest educational level and lowest standard of living" (p. 5). While one would think that Native Americans could continue to live their cultural life-style on the reservations, this possibility has been virtually eliminated by the federal government's establishment of reservations on useless land, forcing Native Americans to live a difficult and impoverished existence. The educational and employment opportunities on reservations are often poor at best, creating a cycle of poverty (Beuf, 1977).

Native Americans have the highest unemployment (40% in 1970) and the lowest average income of any minority group in the United States. The 1970 census revealed that 55% of those on the 24 largest reservations were living below the poverty level. In spite of John Collier's "Indian New Deal" in the 1930s, Glenn Emmons's economic development program in the 1950s, and Lyndon Johnson's "Great Society" of the 1960s, Native Americans still suffer severe problems in the areas of employment, education, income, and health. Unemployment is a result of the geographic isolation of reservations, lack of transportation, lack of skilled labor, and absence of capital. Unemployment on reservations ranged from 20% to more than 70% in 1985 (U.S. Senate, Select Committee on Indian Affairs, 1985). Few industrial jobs are ever available on reservations, and those that become available pay very low wages. In 1983 only 25% of reservation workers earned more than $1,000 a year. In fact, average yearly income for the Native American family was $1,500 in 1983. Off the reservation, racism and lack of education cause high unemployment rates among urban Native Americans (Harrington, 1984).

Unemployment and low income lead to poor housing, malnutrition, and poor community sanitation, which in turn cause health problems. In 1980 the rate of tuberculosis among Native Americans was six times the national average. Native Americans are 70 times more likely to suffer dysentery than Euro-Americans. Their suicide rate is six times that of any other ethnic group, and their alcoholism rate is the highest in the nation. Arrest and incarceration rates are 30 times higher for Native Americans in towns near reservations than for non-Native Americans (Olson & Wilson, 1984).

Unemployment, poverty, and lack of education are all symptoms of the cultural alienation Native Americans experience when trying to live in the dominant culture of the United States. Many of these problems were brought to this continent by the Europeans when they arrived, and are the direct result of oppression of Native Americans.

The land, to Native Americans, could no more be owned or divided than can the air. In traditional culture, the individual worked toward the improvement of the tribe, and the accumulation of material goods for personal use was an offense. Time was seen as a constant. Living in the present was seen as important. Planning for the future or dwelling on the past was futile. These basic cultural views lead to economic "failure" of Native Americans when judged by Anglocentric standards, which value material possession and accumulation, planning for the future, and individual achievement.

History of Oppression

Native Americans have a long history of oppression at the hands of European settlers. As early as 1524, Native Americans were seized by European settlers and sold as slaves in the West Indies. Native Americans were also oppressed by settlers who expected them to adhere to European standards of conduct, cultural values that the Europeans spent little or no time teaching to Native Americans. Disease, slavery, and warfare contributed to the early extinction of many Native American tribes. As the tribes weakened, the Europeans were able to further encroach upon Native American land (Wetmore, 1975). Although the policies and actions of whites toward Native Americans in the nineteenth century appeared to be aimed at termination, it is interesting to note that when a tribe of Native Americans attempted to move into Canada, they were pursued by the cavalry and forced back into the United States. Fueled by the doctrine of Manifest Destiny, whites believed in their divine right to the land and their supremacy over Native Americans (Beuf, 1977; Wetmore, 1975).

Before the arrival of Europeans in North America, there were 2.5 million Native Americans. By the end of the eighteenth century, that number had been reduced to fewer than 250,000. Native Americans were described as vanishing, but they did not vanish. In 1980 there were approximately 1.5 million Native Americans in the United States, and they are now considered to be one of the fastest-growing ethnic groups in the country. There are more than 500 federally recognized and some 365 state-recognized tribes (Olson & Wilson, 1984).

The oppression of Native Americans has continued on the reservation. Native Americans were given land that was believed to be useless. When it was found that some reservation land contained gold or other valuable resources, the land was taken away. In his autobiography, Chief Clinton Rickard (1973) of the Tuscaroras notes that it has become a 200-year-old custom among his people that when gold is discovered on the reservation it is covered up and never spoken of again. Treaties between Native Americans and the federal government were broken by whites more often than they were kept. Disputes over reservation land and boundaries, which are usually settled to the disadvantage of Native Americans, have continued to the present. It has even been proposed that reservation land be broken up and sold to the public at large. Native American tribes seeking official recognition by the federal government often find it a difficult process; often, the end result is that they do not receive official recognition (South, 1980; Wetmore, 1975).

Language and the Arts

We often think of language as merely a set of words, spoken or written, that communicate thoughts. However, many cultures, including the Native American, also have a rich heritage in nonverbal language. One may learn much by "listening" to what Native Americans are expressing through body language, eye movements, silence, and tone of voice (Sue & Sue, 1990). Spoken language varies quite a bit among tribes, with some 150 tribal languages spoken today. One of the methods used by European settlers in referring to groups of Native Americans, along with tribal names, village names, and European geographic names, was by linguistic families (Wetmore, 1975). The Cherokee were the only Native American tribe to develop a written language (South, 1980). While the absence of a written language is often viewed as evidence of the primitive nature of Native Americans and the supremacy of the European settlers, this is a viewpoint taken out of cultural context. Native Americans both live and learn holistically. They learn through listening, by watching others, and through experience. They pass on traditions and customs through oral myths and legends. They live in the present rather than the past or future. When the entire culture is taken into account, it is easy to see that a written language was not necessary for Native Americans until they were forced to interact with the dominant American culture.

The holistic life-style of Native Americans is also reflected in their arts, in their traditions of music, dance, and crafts. Their art is woven throughout the fabric of everyday Native American life and is inseparable from nature, religion, and the universe. The holistic approach of Native American artists can be seen in their methods; in creating a mural, an artist, not using any sketch or outline, paints in all the blue parts first, then all the red, and so forth. It is difficult for linear-thinking individuals to envision being able to approach painting in this manner (South, 1980).

Native American art is best understood from the viewpoint of Native American religious values. The importance Native Americans place on mystical experiences is also central in their art. When these values are kept in mind, one can more easily begin to understand and appreciate Native American art forms. Pottery, masks, basketry, jewelry, weaving, and sculpture are all subject to the regional styles and designs of the hundreds of tribes who engage in creative artistry.

For the Native American, a "work of art" is functional first and foremost, regardless of whether it is aesthetically pleasing to the viewer. Native American painting is seen as an evolutionary process, and it runs the gamut from "primitive" to modern, from traditional to abstract (Wade & Strickland, 1981). Most experts agree that there is remarkable continuity in themes and styles in Native American painting, while at the same time it returns to many of the ancient forms and ideas. This may reflect one of the basic elements of the Native American value system, that the old ways are best and that change only results in problems for the culture.

Racism and Prejudice

Even some of the early European settlers recognized the prejudices of whites toward Native Americans, as evidenced by the following comments of John Lawson, who traveled among and wrote about North Carolina Native Americans:

> They were really better to us than we have been to them, as they always freely give us of their victuals at their quarters, while we let them walk by our doors hungry, and do not often relieve them. We look upon them

with disdain and scorn, and think them little better than beasts in human form; while with all our religion and education, we possess more moral deformities and vices than these people do. (quoted in Rights, 1947, p. 44)

Some hidden or covert prejudice, which may be intentional or unintentional, depending on the source, is seen in the constant message that if Native Americans are to succeed they need to become like whites. The message is that Native Americans and their culture are inferior.

Institutional racism by federal and state governments has been readily apparent over the years through such policies as Manifest Destiny, the loss of Native Americans' citizenship rights of voting and bearing arms under the 1835 North Carolina state constitution, and the relocation of Native Americans under the Indian Removal Act of 1830 (Beuf, 1977; Rickard, 1973).

In a discussion of how children learn about each other, Pang (1991) identifies examples of stereotypes about Native Americans. She cites the use of Native Americans as objects to be counted ("Ten Little Indians"), a practice that usually includes showing identical pictures of Native Americans, from which students conclude that they are a homogeneous population; depicting Native Americans as objects from the past; and the use of Native Americans as mascots for athletic teams. She concludes that these examples "make it seem natural that whites would enjoy some aspects of Indian culture as historic relics, but continue to abrogate treaties with Indians when they 'stand in the way of progress' " (p. 183).

Language is another area in which prejudice can be found. For example, the expressions "Indian giver" and "give it back to the Indians" are used pejoratively. Prejudice is also frequently encountered in the educational system, where school counselors tend to direct Native American students into technical areas and away from college. Studies show the discouraging trend that prejudice toward Native Americans is staying the same or even increasing (Beuf, 1977).

Sociopolitical Factors

Tribal government varies among the tribes. Historically, most tribes were ruled by chiefs and used matriarchal lines of succession. A war chief and council members were usually chosen from among the elders in a tribe (Rights, 1947). Currently, most tribes utilize a tribal council type of government, with variations on whether members are appointed or elected. Some tribes still have chiefs; some are elected and some are hereditary successors. Decisions are usually made either through council consensus or through the spiritual leader.

Native Americans are represented in city, state, and federal governments, but at a lower rate than their proportion of the U.S. population (Rickard, 1973). Native Americans seemed to have relatively little power over their own lives in the United States until the 1960s, when the red power movement brought about positive change and put more power in the hands of Native Americans, primarily through three Native American organizations: the National Indian Youth Council, the National Congress of American Indians, and the American Indian Movement. These changes in social and political power are reflected in the following statement of Chief Clinton Rickard (1973):

> We tried to live in peace, but the government would give us no peace. In the old days the Indian was always going on the warpath to protect his rights. Now in our own day, we still have to go on the warpath. The only thing that has changed is that today we Indians use peaceful weapons. We organize, we write letters, we make speeches, we go to court, we have demonstrations, and we rouse up friendly white people to support us. We are determined to fight to the end for those things that are most precious to us. (p. 137)

The Bureau of Indian Affairs (1988), an agency in the Department of Interior, provides services to approximately 650,000 Native Americans via 123 offices in 12 geographic areas. The BIA provides child welfare services, family services, consultant services, and advisory services to Native American youth and adults. Native American leadership in emerging social and political action movements offers promise for improving social conditions through political activity.

Child-Rearing Practices

Native American children are reared by the extended family, clan, or tribe, with grandparents and other elders usually responsible for teaching the children. Children are given a great deal of freedom and are allowed to explore and be independent quite early in their lives. Disliking a show of temper, Native Americans rarely discipline their children unless real danger exists, believing that a child should be allowed to make mistakes and learn the natural consequences of misbehavior. The elders also do not want ill feelings to arise, as this might prove harmful to the elders in their old age or may offend an ancestral spirit dwelling in the child (Johnson, 1967).

Children develop an inner motivation to learn by "seeking out knowledge of human experience and skills by being present in practice or their telling" (More, 1987, p. 23). The Native American style of child rearing is, therefore, a holistic one that fits in with the rest of the Native American life-style.

Indian parents are generally quite permissive in their training, and children have no fixed schedules for eating or sleeping. Interestingly, among Native American mothers who had attended secondary schools outside their childhood Indian community, changes in this practice have been found that reflect the beliefs and training of the dominant culture. In accordance with their easygoing life-style and attitude toward child rearing, Native American parents do not strike their children. As the child grows, he or she learns to conform to the ideals and beliefs of the tribe; shame and fear become the primary agents in the educational process (More, 1987).

Native American attitudes toward sex are likewise liberal; sex is treated as a part of the natural process of life. Sexual intercourse and facts surrounding it are understood at very early ages. Premarital sexual experiences are common in most Indian villages; in fact, they are so common, they are sometimes thought to be a normal part of the courtship period. When a birth does occur out of wedlock, the tribal community is very protective of the mother, even to the point of finding a husband for her, whether he is the biological father or not. There is no stigma attached to the child, who is loved and cherished along with other children in the tribe (Harrington, 1984).

Religious Practices

To Native Americans, religion is the universe. They believe that almost every act of life is regulated and determined by religion. Some of the early European settlers were able to recognize the holistic quality of Native American religion, despite a general belief that it was "crude"; some commented that there was a completeness and consistency in theory that was beautifully expressed through ceremony and everyday life (Rights, 1947). This holistic view is manifested in the belief in the inseparability of person, nature, and the spirit.

Native Americans' spiritual beliefs are still reflected in and inseparable from their daily lives. Medicine men or shamans are religious men and, commonly, the priests for tribes. Historically, these men have been quite powerful within the tribe; they have been believed to have special powers not possessed by others. Dance, art, and ceremonial festivals are all linked with Native American religious beliefs. In Native American government, councils that cannot reach consensus are not concerned about not making a decision because they believe that such a failure indicates that the time is not right (Brewington, 1959; South, 1980).

Native Americans believe in many gods or spirits, usually with one chief god or "Great Spirit." They worship the forces of nature, such as the sun, wind, water, fire, thunder, and lightning, as well as animals and other spirits. They believe that after death their spirits live on or are reborn in new babies.

Although to non-Native Americans it sometimes seems contradictory, Native Americans have easily accepted and adopted Christianity along with their own beliefs. This acceptance is understandable from the viewpoint of Native American culture, which accepts all religion as part of the universe or "Indian Hoop of Life" (Rights, 1947; Sue, 1981; Sue & Sue, 1990).

Spencer and Jennings (1977) report that the most widespread religion among Native Americans is the "Peyote Cult, whose adherents have been brought together in the Native American Church, which is not the principal religion of the majority of Indians between the Mississippi River and the Rocky Mountains, and is also represented in parts of the Great Basin, southern Canada, and east-central California" (p. 518). The cult combines social ethics and old Indian practices and beliefs. In the ceremonies,

> members consume the nonnarcotic dried buttons of the peyote cactus, which induce visions and hallucinations of varied colors. Although the native components seem to be dominant in the Peyote Cult, it includes also various elements of Christian derivation, such as baptism, the Trinity, the Cross, and other Christian symbolism. At meetings of the cult, there is singing, prayers, and testimonials. (p. 518)

The popularity of the cult seems to spring from the Pan-Indian movement spreading throughout the country, which promotes and extols Native American nationalism and identity through various national organizations. By returning to ancient religious practices, Native Americans affirm the importance of their traditions.

Family Structure and Dynamics

The traditional family form among Native Americans is that of the extended family. In fact, it is probably more appropriate to speak in terms of the clan as the basic family unit. A clan consists of a "group of families or households which traces its descent through the head of the house from a common ancestor" (Wetmore, 1975, p. 116). Many clans trace their ancestry through matrilineal descent. In clans, the female has traditionally been responsible for and performed the duties necessary to preserve the "social organization," usually regulating such matters as punishment, adoption, and marriage (Johnson, 1967; Wetmore, 1975). Clans are often quite large and the birthrate quite high (Beuf, 1977).

Unlike the dominant culture of the United States, which emphasizes youth, the Native American culture values and respects the wisdom and experience of its elders. Thus it is the elders who are responsible for the education of the children and the leadership in the tribe. It is usually the elders who fill positions on tribal councils, where they often serve until their deaths (Wetmore, 1975).

Exact genealogy is not important to Native Americans. Ancestry may be actual or legendary, and might be traced matrilineally or patrilineally. Authority and discipline have had a traditional structure as well. According to Olson and Wilson (1984):

> In a patrilineal family, for example, "grandfather" offered wisdom to everyone; "father" offered authority and responsibility; "uncle" offered assistance; "children" offered obedience; and "brother" offered equality. Since everyone understood the behavior associated with these roles, and most people occupied several roles simultaneously, family values actually governed society, providing direct moral restraints on individual deviancy. (p. 21)

While the characteristics of Native American family structure described above may suggest homogeneity, it is important to recall that there is diversity among Native American families. Just as there is heterogeneity among Native Americans in general, so is there diversity among families, in terms of both structure and function.

Cultural Values and Attitudes

Many of the values and attitudes of Native Americans have already been discussed or alluded to earlier in this chapter. One of the elements of Native American belief that influences these attitudes is the concept of time. To Native Americans, time is not an entity, it just "is." Therefore, they do not worry about or value time, and time is not structured in their everyday lives. Native Americans live in the present. Their belief in immortality—in a soul that lives on or is reborn—and their belief in some individuals' ability to foretell the future while still living in the present (found in some but not all tribes) reflects the interconnectedness of all things and the never-ending cycle of time (Johnson, 1967; Osborne, 1985).

Easily following from the Native American sense of time and holistic culture is the dimension of human activity. The focus of Native Americans is on "being," or existing. They do not worry about obtaining or losing material possessions. Everything that happens is part of the whole and is as it should be. Native Americans will work for a purpose related to "being," and once they fulfill that immediate purpose they will continue to enjoy life as it is (Rights, 1947; Sue, 1981; Sue & Sue, 1990).

The relationship between the individual and nature is one of harmony. Although the supernatural, in the form of spirits, controls the natural world, Native Americans consider that person, nature, and the spirit are all one; all are part of the universe, and all are to live in harmony with one another (Johnson, 1967).

Social relationships are basically collateral. Social relationships exist in the here and now. Although Native Americans do communicate and have relationships with the dead, it is in the form of communicating with spirits of the dead that exist in the present. Often these spirits coexist in the bodies of children (Badwound & Tierney, 1988; Wetmore, 1975).

Native Americans consider human nature to be basically good (although their experiences with the dominant culture may be changing that belief); they act on this belief through their customs of welcoming strangers, sharing with each other, and helping others before self. People who do bad things are seen as inhabited by bad spirits, or perhaps as having had spells put on them. Overall, Native Americans see all people as part of the universe, which should be harmonious as a whole (Johnson, 1967; Matijasic, 1987; Sue, 1981).

Implications

It is clear that educators and counselors wishing to work with Native Americans need preparation beyond the typical classroom experiences offered in colleges and universities. By learning about the Native American culture, one must come to appreciate it, and even to revere it. Oswalt (1978) has this to say about Native Americans:

> Indians themselves are increasingly aware that their cultural identity is important to them, no matter how different it may be from life when whites first arrived. Many Indians seek not just tolerance of their ways but meaningful moral and financial support in order that their identity may endure so long as the waters shall flow and the sun shall shine. This is their clear right and our abiding obligation because this land indeed was theirs. (p. 549)

In a study reported by Tamminen, Smaby, Powless, and Gum (1980) at the University of Minnesota, Native Americans with a history of alcoholism and drug dependency were paired with Native American counselors who were familiar with and concerned about the problems of drugs and alcoholism. Because Native Americans frequently find it difficult to accept help from non-Native Americans, this pilot program was designed to attract and prepare Native Americans to be counselors through a paraprofessional counseling program. During the first three years, 62 of the 78 individuals who started the program completed it, and the researchers reported it to be successful.

Another study, by Dauphinais, LaFromboise, and Rowe (1980), showed that Native American high school students rated Native Americans as more effective than non-Native Americans in counseling situations. Reflecting this, a nondirective, facilitative verbal response style was seen as less effective than either a directive or cultural/experiential style. These findings are noteworthy given that 55% of Native Americans do not return for counseling after an initial interview, compared with 30% of the general population.

Johnson and Lashley (1989) found that the degree of commitment to Native American culture affects preferences for counselors from a particular ethnic group. Those with strong cultural commitments expect more "nurturance, facilitative conditions, and counselor expertise than those with a weak commitment" (p. 120).

According to Hodge (1981), there are three Native American reactions to white-dominated society. His typology defines these three groups (bicultural, traditional, and marginal) in terms of Indian identity development. Sue and Sue (1990) use a worldview orientation that involves personal control and responsibility. The Hodge and Sue perspectives can be combined to promote greater understanding of Native Americans.

First, individuals resembling the bicultural type emulate many white pursuits, such as wealth, formal education, and recreation. They attempt to obtain these material benefits through hard work and through manipulating politics and industry. These Native Americans compete in economic and political affairs of the dominant culture while maintaining their cultural heritage. They believe their efforts can effect change. They are self-reliant, possess a strong desire to overcome racial barriers, and value achievement.

Traditional Native Americans distrust whites in the dominant culture. This results from past conflicts and value differences between the two cultures. They use their "Indianness" to avoid whites and the white life-style. Such Native Americans pursue wealth only as a means of escaping white domination. They want to perpetuate their native culture. Many fit the internal control-external responsibility worldview. They realistically perceive barriers of discrimination, yet they believe in their ability to improve their current conditions. They wish to maintain their identity, and sometimes their actions are militant.

Marginal Native Americans do not attempt to compete with the dominant culture. They have an exchange system involving goods, rights, obligations, and emotional support. They accept the dominant culture, believing that they are unable to have any impact on the established order. They expect the government to provide housing and financial assistance. Many resemble the external control-external responsibility worldview. They maintain a low profile and expect the dominant culture to provide for their needs; they may be said to have developed "learned helplessness."

After gaining awareness of Native American culture, helping professionals can incorporate this awareness into educational and counseling theory. Theorists have concluded that Native Americans value trustworthiness and understanding within the counseling relationship. Thomason (1991) suggests a number of strategies for those who anticipate counseling interventions with Native Americans, including the following:

(1) Become familiar with Native American ideas about healing.
(2) Learn as much as possible about the client's specific tribe and tribal beliefs.
(3) Meet the client as a person rather than as a case.
(4) Follow the client's lead in regard to nonverbal behavior.
(5) Employ a fairly active and directive problem-solving approach (this will be effective with many clients, but bear in mind that other approaches may be useful as well).
(6) Maintain the options of involving the family of the client, visiting the home of the client, or involving a traditional healer in the counseling process.

Educators must be honest and accepting, and must respect both individual Native Americans and the Native American culture. It is not enough merely to assert that one is culturally sensitive and aware of Native American values. Rather, educators and counselors must develop approaches that have demonstrated utility with Native Americans in a variety of settings.

Questions for Review and Reflection

(1) What has been the major impact of Native American culture on the dominant culture of the United States?
(2) What Native American cultural trait is most similar to a trait in the dominant culture? Which is most different? How do these similarities and differences influence or hinder interactions between Native Americans and the dominant culture?
(3) What image comes to your mind when you think of "Native American"? How does (or can) this image influence your interactions with Native Americans? How does Hodge's (1981) three-group typology of Native American worldviews help educators or counselors understand specific individuals in the culture?
(4) What is the relationship between the attempts at forced acculturation for Native Americans and the subsequent treatment of Native Americans living on reservations?

(5) What similarities and differences are likely to be evident between reservation and nonreservation Native Americans? How can these similarities and differences be used in working with Native American students or clients?

(6) What impact does "Indian time" have on Native Americans in the dominant culture? How can educators or counselors use this concept of time in working with Native American students or clients?

(7) What impact does traditional body language of Native Americans have on their interactions with the dominant culture? How can educators or counselors prevent miscommunication in these encounters?

(8) Describe the cultural value that influences Native American art. What impact does this view toward art have on other Native American cultural values?

(9) What is the meaning of the phrase "Indian giver"? In what ways do you think the use of the phrase influences Native American interactions with the dominant culture?

(10) How do Native Americans' relationships with and respect for the elderly influence the way they interact with nature and with other people?

References

Badwound, E., & Tierney, W. G. (1988). Leadership and American Indian values: The tribal college dilemma. *Journal of American Indian Education, 28,* 9-15.

Beuf, A. H. (1977). *Red children in white America.* University Park: University of Pennsylvania Press.

Brewington, C. D. (1959). *The five civilized Indian tribes of eastern North Carolina.* Clinton, NC: Bass.

Bureau of Indian Affairs. (1988). *American Indians today.* Washington, DC: Author.

Dauphinais, P., LaFromboise, T., & Rowe, W. (1980). Perceived problems and sources of help for American Indian students. *Counselor Education and Supervision, 20,* 37-44.

Foreman, L. D. (1987). Curricular choice in the age of self-determination. *Journal of American Indian Education, 26,* 1-6.

Harrington, M. (1984). *The new American poverty.* New York: Holt, Rinehart & Winston.

Hirschfelder, A. (1982). *Happily may I walk: American Indians and Alaska natives today.* New York: Scribner's.

Hodge, W. H. (1981). *The first Americans.* New York: Holt, Rinehart & Winston.

Johnson, F. R. (1967). *The Tuscaroras: Mythology-medicine-culture.* Murfreesboro, NC: Johnson.

Johnson, M. E., & Lashley, K. H. (1989). Influence of Native-Americans' cultural commitment on preferences for counselor ethnicity and expectations about counseling. *Journal of Multicultural Counseling and Development, 17,* 115-122.

Matijasic, T. D. (1987). Reflected values: Sixteenth-century Europeans view the Indians of North America. *American Indian Culture and Research Journal, 11*, 31-50.

More, A. J. (1987). Native Indian learning styles: A review for researchers and teachers. *Journal of American Indian Education, 27*, 17-28.

O'Connell, J. C. (1985). A family systems approach for serving rural, reservation Native American communities. *Journal of American Indian Education, 24*, 1-6.

Olson, J. S., & Wilson, R. (1984). *Native Americans in the twentieth century.* Provo, UT: Brigham Young University Press.

Osborne, B. (1985). Research into Native American's cognition: 1973-1982. *Journal of American Indian Education, 24*, 9-24.

Oswalt, W. H. (1978). *This land was theirs: A study of North American Indians.* New York: John Wiley.

Pang, V. O. (1991). Teaching children about social issues: Kidpower. In C. L. Sleeter (Ed.), *Empowerment through multicultural education* (pp. 179-197). Albany: State University of New York.

Pertusati, L. (1988). Beyond segregation or integration: A case study from effective Native American education. *Journal of American Indian Education, 27*, 11-20.

Rickard, C. C. (1973). *Fighting Tuscarora: Autobiography of Chief Clinton Rickard.* New York: Syracuse University.

Rights, D. L. (1947). *The American Indian in North Carolina.* Durham, NC: Duke University Press.

South, S. A. (1980). *Indians in North Carolina.* Raleigh: North Carolina Department of Cultural Resources, Division of Archives and History.

Spencer, R. R., & Jennings, J. D. (1977). *The Native Americans: Ethnology and backgrounds of American Indians.* New York: Harper & Row.

Stock, L. (1987). Native Americans: A brief profile. *Journal of Visual Impairment and Blindness, 81*, 152.

Sue, D. W. (1981). *Counseling the culturally different: Theory and practice.* New York: John Wiley.

Sue, D. W., & Sue, D. (1990). *Counseling the culturally different: Theory and practice* (2nd ed.). New York: John Wiley.

Tamminen, A. W., Smaby, M. H., Powless, R. E., & Gum, M. F. (1980). Preparing Native American counselors for the chemically dependent Native American. *Counselor Education and Supervision, 19*, 310-317.

Thomason, T. C. (1991). Counseling Native Americans: An introduction for non-Native American counselors. *Journal of Counseling and Development, 69*, 321-327.

U.S. Senate, Select Committee on Indian Affairs. (1985). *Indian juvenile alcoholism and eligibility for BIA schools* (Senate Hearing 99-286). Washington, DC: Government Printing Office.

Wade, E. L., & Strickland, R. (1981). *Magic images.* Norman: University of Oklahoma.

Washburn, W. E. (1975). *The Indian in America.* New York: Harper & Row.

Wetmore, R. Y. (1975). *First on the land: The North Carolina Indians.* Winston-Salem, NC: John F. Blair.

Yates, A. (1987). Current status and future directions of research on the American Indian child. *American Journal of Psychiatry, 9*, 1135-1142.

5

Japanese Americans

As Japan is moving into a position to dominate the world economy in the twenty-first century, it is imperative that we look carefully at how the Japanese and Japanese Americans influence the dominant culture of the United States. An advertiser's recent campaign to buy only products "made in the U.S.A." supports the contention that many in the dominant culture of the United States feel threatened, resentful, and suspicious of the Japanese. Japanese technology has outstripped that of the United States, causing negative feelings to persist. The Japanese economy is highly industrialized and, technologically speaking, is giving industries in the United States fierce competition. In its February 4, 1988, issue, *Newsweek* reported on a Gallup Poll that showed that 50% of those in the United States favored trade barriers in certain industries that would make it difficult or expensive to sell foreign imports here; 46% felt that Asian-American students were winning an increasing number of academic awards and scholarships (see Powell & Martin, 1988).

Given this impact on the dominant culture of the United States, we need to be aware of the Japanese not only in economic terms, but in cultural terms as well. In analyzing the Japanese community in the United States, one must review the changes throughout history from generation to generation. The first Japanese to migrate to the United States, whether they settled in cities or in rural areas, sought out other Japanese. This caused them to fashion a unique mode of community life in their efforts to adjust to the conditions in a new environment while maintaining their traditional values. One may describe the Japanese-American family and community prior to World War II as an immigrant group trying to become established in a new country.

Acculturation

The degree of acculturation to the dominant culture can range from minimal to full acculturation. Each succeeding generation of Japanese-Americans has been known by the Japanese word for that generation, a unique practice among immigrant groups. This naming of generations is the Japanese way of honoring those who came to the United States.

First-generation Japanese, the generation that immigrated to the United States, are known as *Issei* (literally "first generation" in Japanese). These immigrants were tightly bound to the traditions of their homeland, tended to live in segregated communities, and upheld their Japanese identity. Interestingly, the Issei experienced more psychological stress and were more externally controlled than subsequent generations. They also had lower self-esteem than some of the later-generation Japanese Americans (Padilla, Wagatsuma, & Lindholm, 1985). The Issei essentially resisted acculturation.

The second generation, or *Nisei,* were more acculturated than the Issei. They were less psychologically stressed and more internally controlled than the Issei, but had lower self-esteem. This might be due to the fact that they were taught through the media and schools about individuality, freedom, and other dominant culture values but at home were infused with the quite different traditional Japanese values of their Issei parents. Montero (1981) found that on every indicator of assimilation (visiting patterns with relatives, ethnicity of two closest friends, ethnicity of favorite organization, and ethnicity of spouse) it is the socioeconomically successful Nisei who are most assimilated and cut off from the ethnic community. According to Tomine (1991), this intensified urgency toward acculturation was the result of "questioned loyalty" and "wartime hysteria."

The *Kibei* (who are technically Nisei) find themselves in the unique position of being outside both the Japanese and the dominant culture. They are the mid-generation Japanese whose Nisei parents sent them to Japan to school between their eighth and fourteenth years and then brought them back to the United States. They were ostracized by the Japanese and rejected by the dominant culture of the United States.

Wilson and Hosokawa (1980) show that the dilemma in which the Kibei found themselves was dependent on the age at which they were sent to Japan, the length of time they remained there, and the educational practices in place at the time they were there. Some returned to the United States with anti-American attitudes, while others returned and adjusted easily. Both groups were less proficient in English than the Nisei who had remained in the United States. During World War II, according to Wilson and Hosokawa, "hundreds of Kibei provided an invaluable service as instructors in military language-training programs, as interpreters and translators in the Pacific theater, and psychological warfare specialists" (p. 167).

The *Sansei* youth, or third generation, have the highest degree of acculturation. Reared by the assimilation-oriented Nisei, they are driven to prove themselves, to succeed and excel in the dominant culture. Padilla et al. (1985) found the Sansei to have higher self-esteem, lower stress, and higher internality than the two previous generations. It may be assumed that many Sansei demonstrate what is called the "Hansen effect." Hansen (1952) has pointed out that while some might view third-generation persons as acculturated, many have retained their ethnic identity and express an intense interest in their families' backgrounds and histories. It seems reasonable to expect the fourth generation (*Yonsei*) and the fifth generation (*Gosei*) to have even higher degrees of acculturation than previous generations. What might be viewed as acculturation of these groups may actually be biculturalism, or the ability to behave according to a particular value system depending on the situation.

While initially it was said that the Japanese could not be assimilated because of their "vile habits, low standard of living, extremely high birthrate, and so on" (Chuman, 1976, p. 74), there has been very little opposition to acculturation by Japanese Americans. Certainly there has been no militant or blatant opposition. In keeping with the Japanese emphasis on education and social status, acculturation has been "rewarded" by the dominant culture.

Poverty and Economic Concerns

In Japan, schools at the primary and secondary level have assumed such importance in determining an individual's future that chances of acquiring higher status are virtually decided before one is barely out of the teenage years. Schooling is critical because social advancement for most Japanese means joining the ranks of white-collar workers in one of the country's giant corporations. As Nakane (1972) reports, once a person gets such a job—known in Japan as becoming a "salary man"—he can generally count on remaining with the company for life. During his career promotions come regularly; he can usually predict when he will become the head of a department or assistant to a manager. Except during periods of unusual economic turmoil, employees are seldom discharged or laid off.

To obtain a corporate job that will set him up for life, however, the aspirant must be a graduate of one of the better universities. The difficult stage in the individual's career is passing the examinations that qualify him for the limited positions open in the universities. The psychological toll of such early status competition is marked by an alarming number of suicides among children who despair over their academic prospects.

Jenkins (1973) conducted a study on blue- and white-collar democracy in other countries and found that in Japan the man is known by the company that keeps him. Joining a large corporation upon leaving school, the Japanese youth expects to stay with the firm for his entire working life, never to be fired except for criminal acts or on grounds of insanity. In return, he is expected to work loyally, to identify with the corporation, to follow the rules, and to wait his turn for promotion. The Japanese worker derives not only his livelihood and security from his place in the corporation, but also health care, further education, and social life. Every large corporation also has a semiformal system to ensure that the employee's assignments match his personal needs and career desires as much as possible. If he is a young man seeking to marry, the company stands ready to help him find a bride and to provide a priest and a hall for the wedding ceremony.

This kind of lifelong dependency on a single organization clearly does not fit Western traditions of mobility and diversity. In the United States one finds a somewhat different educational and occupational pattern of development among Japanese Americans. Though the "model minority" label often attached to them is considered inaccurate by some experts, Japanese Americans do constitute a group that seems to have "made it" as far as educational attainment is concerned. According to *Newsweek on Campus,* "One-third of all Asian-Americans aged 25 and over had attended college for four or more years, compared with 17.1 percent of Caucasians and 8.4 Black . . . and . . . Asian-Americans far outdistance every other minority in the country academically" ("The Drive to Excel," 1984, p. 4).

In 1971, *Newsweek* reported that these students represent the fastest-growing segment in American universities, where they dominate mathematics, engineering, and science courses ("Success Story," 1971). Also, they outperformed all other ethnic groups on the math section of the Scholastic Aptitude Test, and rated slightly lower than Caucasians on the verbal section. A study by Chu (1971) found that 68.2% of Japanese-American males studied engineering or the physical sciences. Lack of English-language skills may lead some Japanese Americans into disciplines requiring a minimum of self-expression. Several possible reasons have been given for the movement of Japanese Americans into the physical sciences: deficiency in language skills (Kagiwada & Fujimote, 1973; Kaneshige, 1973; Sue & Kirk, 1972; Watanabe, 1973); cultural injunctions that restrict self-expression (Kagiwada & Fujimote, 1973; Sue & Kirk, 1972; Sue & Sue, 1973; Watanabe, 1973); and pressure from Japanese-American families, which direct their children into areas where they have the best chance of succeeding, and from educators and counselors, who unthinkingly place Asian students in courses that minimize English and maximize mathematical skills (Watanabe, 1973). Sue and Sue (1973) address the issue of this success myth about Asians, pointing out that it seems to serve three purposes:

(1) It represents an attempt to reaffirm the belief that any group, regardless of race, creed, or color, can succeed in a "democratic" society if they work hard enough.
(2) It has operated to create friction between Asians and other cultural groups.
(3) It has discouraged and/or prevented Asian Americans from obtaining needed moral and financial assistance from educational institutions, business, government, and industry.

Whether because the technical occupational fields offer more career potential or because of they do indeed have a propensity for mathematical and physical science fields, it would appear that Asian Americans with college degrees are entering the more concrete, structured, and detailed occupations. Less movement by Japanese Americans is seen in the social sciences, which stress the higher verbal skills. Kagiwada and Fujimote (1973) found that job discrimination even among the well educated with considerable experience is still practiced. Considered unsuitable for upper-echelon positions by some prejudiced personnel officers, Japanese Americans are often passed over for promotions. Another important point is that not all Asian Americans have attained higher education. Many earn modest incomes and work long hours in family-owned laundries, restaurants, other small businesses, and farm enterprises.

History of Oppression

Japanese immigrants began coming to the United States in large numbers around 1890. They were at once subjected to the punishment and harassment already known to the Chinese. This "anti-Oriental" atmosphere was the result of the fear and ignorance summed up in the phrase "the yellow peril." Chuman (1976) describes the propaganda against the Japanese:

Through exaggerated reports of the number of Japanese entering America and their control or use of agricultural lands or through outright expressions of hatred for them, the agitators made a case that the apparently peaceful Japanese immigrants were in truth the sinister vanguard of an invading horde, bent solely on the conquest of the country. (p. 74)

Sue and Sue (1990) conclude that because Japan was a rising international power, the anti-Japanese feeling did not manifest itself directly in legislation to restrict immigration, but led to a "gentlemen's agreement" to stem the flow of Asians to the United States. To harass the Japanese further, California in 1913 passed the Alien Land Law, which forbade aliens to own land. The Alien Land Law was an emotional warning to the public that Japanese farmers were going to take over agricultural land. In fact, the Japanese owned only 12,726 farm acres out of 11 million acres in California in 1912 (Chuman, 1976).

After the devastating attack on Pearl Harbor on December 7, 1941, all Japanese living in the United States came under extreme suspicion. Thousands of Japanese Americans were rounded up and "contraband" such as cameras, flashlights, and hunting rifles were confiscated. These events were reported prominently by the news media, but the fact that none of those apprehended had done anything to harm the national interest was largely ignored. A total of 110,000 Japanese Americans were sent to concentration camps. They accepted their internment with virtually no resistance; imprisoned for no crime but their race, they met their fate with resignation, a primary characteristic of Japanese culture.

Even though at least 50% of the citizens of the United States viewed the average Japanese American as loyal, after their release it was an uphill battle for Japanese Americans to readjust and adapt to the environment after the war. Prewar competitors of Japanese-American produce wholesalers founded the American League of California, which urged Japanese Americans to demonstrate their patriotism by "remaining away from the Pacific Coast" (Petersen, 1971). Bumper stickers proclaiming "No Japs Wanted in California" were popular. Until the beginning of 1946, the Teamsters Union boycotted Japanese-American-grown produce. The California Board of Equalization issued no commercial licenses to Japanese Americans until the War Relocation Authority threatened to initiate legal action.

According to Kitano (1976), elderly Japanese Americans were beaten down and afraid. Most settled in trailer parks off the beaten path. For a decade after World War II, Japanese Americans found housing to be the most significant area of discrimination against them. Japanese Americans were also often underemployed in terms of their educational backgrounds, occupational skills, potential, and economic aspirations. It was common for Nisei with degrees from U.S. colleges and universities to be found in underpaid, menial, unskilled work because they were denied employment in the fields for which they had been trained.

Language and the Arts

Many Japanese-American families still speak Japanese at home but communicate well in English outside the home. Many other differences in styles of communication between Japanese culture and the dominant culture in the

United States are nonverbal. For instance, there is very little eye contact among Japanese. Direct eye contact is considered impolite and even disrespectful toward seniors. Minimal eye contact takes place only among families and peers.

In Japan, there is a maximum amount of body contact between mother and child, including sleeping together. Young teenagers might hold hands, but hugging and kissing are considered to be in poor taste. After childhood, there is no body contact with others except that between husband and wife, which occurs only in total privacy.

Instead of shaking hands, the Japanese traditionally bow. The depth of the bow indicates the social position of the person being greeted. A complete bow is made when one is looking at a shrine. Upon encountering an old friend or relative he or she has not seen in a long time, a Japanese bows many times.

Since physical space is limited in Japan, the amount of "personal space" individuals are comfortable with around them is smaller than in the United States. Taking up a large personal space is interpreted as rude and hostile.

For Japanese, earth and heaven meet through people to form art. Art is elegant and even reverent, yet simple and easily handled. It is usually linear and nonrepetitive; it has one theme and definite closure. Often, art in the form of paintings, screens, scrolls, and clothing are characterized by bright colors and subjects of nature and/or people. The cultural emphasis on silence and reservation of verbal communication can be seen in the classical dance-drama form known as *Noh,* in which actors wearing masks exchange little or no verbal dialogue. The martial arts stress relaxation, deflection, and the interaction of mind and body as sources of inner strength in defending against an outside aggressor. Other important Japanese art forms that combine spiritual and aesthetic experience are *ikebana* (flower arranging), gardening, and the intense and highly stylized tea ceremony.

Racism and Prejudice

Japanese Americans have experienced intense racism, discrimination, and prejudice in the United States. Early Japanese Americans were ambitious and industrious, expecting upward mobility and the "American dream." Kitano (1976) points out that even though these ideals were similar to those found in the dominant culture, it was the ambition and striving of the Japanese Americans that drew suspicion and resentment from the dominant culture.

Prejudice and discrimination left over from the "Chinese problem" created an "anti-Asian" atmosphere. During World War II, the print media incited racial violence against the Japanese by alleging espionage and sabotage (Okihiro & Sly, 1983). The press fostered the notion of the "yellow peril," creating a climate of intolerance and racism. Sue (1981) characterizes the wartime relocation of Japanese Americans as the most blatant evidence of prejudice and discrimination.

Okihiro and Sly (1983) have suggested that very few of the Sansei have felt the demoralizing agony of anti-Japanese prejudice and racism. Most Sansei have grown up in homes unmarked by a noticeable cultural division between Japan and the United States. They have benefited from the material success of their parents and the physical labor of their grandparents. They have received parental support for their educational pursuits without difficulty. Henkin (1985) describes the subtle forms of racism and prejudice that are felt by the Sansei:

> Outside the home, the Sansei live very much in the heart of American culture. They may feel American, speak American, act American, and think American. But unlike their friends in the cultural mainstream, they can never look American, and as far as America is concerned, then, there is some important way in which they can never be American. The tacit prejudice that is often unacknowledged and even unperceived dogs their steps and generates confusion about the Sansei's identity. (p. 502)

According to Kitano (1976), there are elements of a "schizophrenic adaptation" on the part of Japanese Americans to life in the United States. He adds that this is true of most other physically identifiable groups as well. The dilemma of how to behave when interacting with the dominant culture and how to behave when interacting with one's own group is a major concern for members of diverse cultures. The fact is that Japanese Americans are trying to achieve acceptance in a culture where the terms of citizenship, social status, and economic well-being are often racially determined.

Sociopolitical Factors

The Japanese-American social structure has often been described as vertical rather than horizontal, meaning that relations are clearly defined to those above or below in the social hierarchy. The lack of political activity among Japanese Americans can be explained through a close examination of these values. Japanese Americans value maintaining low visibility and conformity in order not to bring negative attention to themselves. A model Japanese leader is one who is informed, possesses thorough knowledge, and yet avoids the spotlight.

The Japanese American Citizen's League (JACL), the only national organization for the Japanese, began in the early 1920s in response to the special interests and problems of Japanese Americans. Given little choice, the organization cooperated with the evacuation and internment orders of World War II. The JACL reorganized after the war and redefined its goals and functions. The organization maintains lobbies in Washington, lodges legal protests, and generally protects and assists Japanese Americans. The JACL spearheaded the recent successful movement to gain reparations for those interned during World War II.

The Japanese-American community has served to hold Japanese Americans together by reinforcing values, customs, behaviors, and social control. According to Kitano (1976):

> The most pressing reason of the Japanese Americans for maintaining their own social groups revolves around the problem of dating and marriage. "Do you want your daughter to marry one?" is a question that is asked not only by the majority group but also by ethnic parents. This concern has led to the development and maintenance of many Japanese organizations. (p. 113)

In general, Japanese Americans have achieved high socioeconomic mobility in spite of discrimination against them. The value system of the Japanese encouraged economic success and educational opportunity and further opened the door to higher occupational status.

To work effectively with Japanese individuals in the United States, educators and counselors must be aware of and understand Japanese customs and values and must comprehend several aspects of the Japanese personality. A Judo Shinto priest attests to the enigmatic nature of the Japanese personality when he states, "It takes 20 generations to mold a Japanese, i.e., to inculcate the essence of order, obedience, and conformity" (Masuda, Matsumoto, & Meredith, 1970).

Child-Rearing Practices

In Japan, as well as among Japanese Americans, elders are viewed with great respect, and a strong family system is very important. According to Garfinkle (1983), the dominant orientation of the Japanese family begins with the constant interest and pressure that the Japanese mother provides for her children. The Japanese mother devotes herself to the rearing of her children and pushes them to excel academically. The intensely close relationship between mother and child shows the most pervasive values of Japanese society; the work ethic, selflessness, and group endeavor. When it comes to the discipline of children, the Japanese mother is more inclined than the American mother to appeal to feelings as a coercive tool, by simply expressing her displeasure. Japanese writers on child rearing recommend mildness in the direct verbal teaching of children. They believe that children should be admonished in a firm but calm manner, and that adults should not use abusive language or show anger and impatience. A study by Kurokawa (1968) with Japanese-American families showed that the Japanese mother rocks the child more and talks less, while the American mother talks more and touches less. The mean age for independence training was 8.9 for Sanseis and 6.78 for Caucasians. According to Nancy Shand, an anthropologist at the Menninger Foundation, an expression used to describe Japanese mothers is *Kyoiku-Mama,* which translates to "education mommy." Perhaps the social prestige of motherhood among the Japanese is one reason for the critical difference in child-rearing patterns ("The Drive to Excel," 1984).

According to anthropologist Ruth Benedict (1945), the Japanese father is less of a disciplinarian than are fathers in almost any Western nation. To the Japanese father, the child may show only respect. The father is the great exemplar to the child, of high hierarchical position, and the child must learn to express the proper respect to him "for training." Sue (1981) and Watanabe (1973) also describe the family system as patriarchal, with the father's authority unquestioned. The primary duty of a son is allegiance to his father, before his obligations to be a good husband and father to his own children. Subservience to males is the female role in the family, along with the performance of domestic duties and education of the children.

Religious Practices

Japanese churches have played a significant role in the development of community solidarity and cohesion. Most of the first Japanese who came to the United States were Buddhists. Buddhism is closely tied to the family system so revered in Japanese culture. Many sacred rites are performed at a family shrine. Faith is renewed on a day-to-day basis, with observances conducted within the family. Buddhism encourages the awareness of Japanese values and heritage. From Confucianism came the standard of social behavior that dictates respect and obedience for authority and for elders. Henkin (1985) explains how the Buddhist/Confucian/Shintoist background of the Japanese culture in Japan has established a perceptual, conceptual, and behavioral ground of being that advocates inner discipline and encourages people to conceal frustrations and disappointments. Also, they are expected to submerge individual concerns, to recognize filial piety and moral obligations to others as superior to personal desires, and to persist in their tasks in the face of unhappiness despite the probability of failure or defeat.

The Christian churches in the United States attracted many immigrants who were seeking cultural belonging and economic advancement. The structure of the Japanese Christian church was fitted to the needs of the Japanese family. However, variations in religious practices reflected age and generational differences among the Japanese Americans. The concerns of the Issei are geared to the needs of the aged. The majority of Issei attend Buddhist and Christian churches in large numbers and appear to be seeking comfort and reassurance in the face of old age and death. The Nisei, on the other hand, have very different concerns. Their social status is likely to influence their patterns of church attendance. Thus there seems to be no universal concern with religion among Japanese Americans. Loyalties are instead to the home, the family, and related specific groups.

Cultural emphases on money, education, and group conformity do not come from religion as much as from the geography and history of Japan. The standard of group cooperation grew out of Japan's being a rice-growing country. During the days of the feudal system and afterwards, the neighborhood had to work together, because survival depended upon it. Even though Japan now has a large urban population, these values are still upheld. Also, because Japan is such a small island, there is fierce competition for jobs. Thus the geography of the land dictates the almost obsessive value the culture places on education and money—not religion. The values of group conformity and social status via education and money are very much a part of the lives of Japanese Americans as well.

Family Structure and Dynamics

Consistent with the value of respect for authority and elders, one finds among Japanese Americans values of allegiance to the family and dependency versus individualism and self-reliance. Whether children are taught the reciprocal family obligation as shared family values or, as Watanabe (1973) asserts, because of racism in the United States that forces family members to rely on each other for personal security, the fact remains that Japanese Americans find themselves duty bound and obligated to the family. According to Kaneshige (1973), internal conflicts of any family members are resolved only within the family system. To display to outsiders that there are problems is to bring disgrace to the family name. Related to this concept of shame, or the avoidance of bringing disgrace to the family name, is the idea that the individual is of minimal importance. Belief that one exists only in relation to one's group seriously conflicts with the concept of reaching individual self-fulfillment. To do so would be to display attributes of selfishness and exaggerated self-importance (Kaneshige, 1973). Sue and Sue

(1973) state that the Japanese tendency toward perseverance as role perfectionism is one of the prime motivators of Japanese children and their mothers. This type of motivator has the effect of exhorting Japanese to endure experiences with a stoic attitude. The Japanese mother-child relationship may be summarized in one word, *amae,* an attitude toward people characterized by affection, feelings of dependency, and the expectation of an emotionally satisfying response. This means that love is combined with a strong sense of reciprocal obligation and dependence. Watanabe (1973) also identifies the learned family trait of indirect communication versus direct communication. Clearly defined roles of dominance and deference virtually rule out argument and debate. Communication flows one way, from parent to child. Direct messages predominate, and exchanges are generally brief and perfunctory.

One area of extensive contrast between the Japanese and Japanese Americans might be found in the institution of marriage. According to Ravich and Wyden (1974), in Japan, matchmakers engaged by parents were still arranging more than a third of all marriages during the early 1970s. Postwar Japan has seen the development of a more impersonal matchmaker, the marriage bureau. Run sometimes by private operators, sometimes by government agencies, the new bureaus ask applicants about their income, health, and attitudes before arranging a meeting between two possibly congenial young people. The giant Mitsubishi company set up a marriage service of its own, using a computer to match employees who wanted to find mates and were willing to pay a fee for promising leads. This service cut down the time and money employees would otherwise spend finding partners. According to Benedict (1945), the Japanese set up no ideal, as do members of the dominant U.S. culture, about love and marriage as one and the same thing. The Japanese regard the real aim of marriage as procreation, and feel that love takes time to develop during the family life. The rate of divorce in Japan is low. If, in fact, there is a divorce, the wife usually loses everything, including her children, and returns to her own family in shame. If a Japanese husband can afford it, he often will keep a mistress. The mistress is not added to his family but is set up in her own home. Only in exceptional cases—for instance, when the mistress has a child—does he bring her into his home, and then she is usually treated as one of the servants. This practice crosses all class lines among the Japanese, with economics being the determining factor as to the status of the woman chosen for a mistress.

In Western cultures and among most Japanese Americans, marriage for love is the ideal. In a study by Nishio (1982) of characteristics of Japanese and Japanese Americans, about one-half of the Japanese Americans sampled had been married to non-Japanese. He also found divorce rates higher among Japanese Americans than among the Japanese in Japan. Kikumura and Kitano (1973) and Tinker (1973) found that for such areas as Los Angeles,

San Francisco, and Fresno, California, the incidence of Japanese-American interracial marriage had approached 50% as of the time of their studies. Presumably this is a measure of the success of acculturation of the Japanese and the non-Japanese. Certainly these interracial experiences present an arena for possible conflict for those of Japanese ancestry.

Cultural Values and Attitudes

In the traditional Japanese ethical system, the central value is duty—social obligation and social responsibility. In fact, the foundation of the ethical system is the notion of collective obligations. According to Smith and Beardsley (1962), there is a strong emphasis on "collaterality" in interpersonal relations, which stresses the welfare of the group and consensus among its members.

Another Japanese value is the concept of *enryo* (reserve, constraint), which helps to explain many differences in style of communication and behavior (Smith & Beardsley, 1962). The concept originally referred to the deferential way in which "inferiors" were to act toward "superiors." One manifestation of *enryo* is the use of silence as a safe response to an embarrassing or ambiguous situation. Japanese Americans often adapt *enryo* to their interactions with members of the dominant culture. The interaction rules related to *enryo* are learned within the family, where a child is taught the importance of reticence, modesty, indirect communication, and humility. The child is taught to be sensitive to reactions of others and is punished for boastful, aggressive, and self-centered behavior.

Conformity is another value that stresses conventional behavior and strict allegiance to rules and regulations (Kitano, 1976). This value often leads to the development of dependent personalities. Many Japanese believe that suffering and hard work are necessary ingredients of character building. Finally, the Japanese place a great deal of emphasis on status distinction, so that sex, class, age, caste, family, lineage, and other variables of social status are vital to the culture.

Being future oriented and concerned about the welfare of their children, the Japanese value education. In fact, the Japanese educational system may be the most effective in the world. The estimated illiteracy rate in Japan is less than 1%. One of the most powerful forces for uniformity in education is derived from the Japanese reluctance to stigmatize or embarrass anyone publicly. There is no tracking in Japanese elementary and secondary schools. Students of varying abilities study in the same classes. Automatic promotion is the unchallenged rule throughout the nine years that Japanese children are required to attend school. Academic competition is intense because an individual's social status depends heavily on which university he or she attends.

The Japanese values and norms most likely to endure are those that intersect with the relative power position of Japanese in the United States. Many of these are consistent with the stereotypical traits associated with Japanese Americans by those in the dominant culture: quiet, conforming, loyal, diligent, good citizens, high achievers in education, group oriented, indirect communicators, respectful of hierarchy, submissive (if female), dependent on family, and having a high sense of family obligation. These values are in contrast to the dominant culture values of individual self-realization, high verbal participation, female assertiveness, challenge of authority, and a more egalitarian system of family dynamics.

Implications

Of special importance, as Motet (1981) points out, is to differentiate between the Japanese resident who is returning to Japan and the Japanese-American citizen. How can we make for a good adjustment and yet not cause reentry problems for the alien eventually returning to Japan? The answer is to pursue a course of cultural enrichment rather than cultural change. To ask that the Japanese adopt dominant-culture values would be inappropriate. The helper role in this case might be more that of a translator of differences between the two cultures, an informational resource. In order to help Japanese students and their families function efficiently, and to broaden their perspective on both cultures, helping professionals need to have an understanding of areas such as the following:

(1) the differences in values and customs of the two cultures

(2) the Japanese values of respect for hierarchy and authority, elder orientation, submissive role of women, role of the Japanese mother in educating the children, indirect rather than direct communication, and family dependence and dynamics

(3) the difficulties of reentry for Japanese families returning to Japan, especially for the children, who have probably become more acculturated into the dominant U.S. culture

(4) the dependency of the family, when applicable, on the corporation where the father is employed

(5) the need for the helping professional to serve as an information source on Japanese values and customs for those who interact with the Japanese in the United States

(6) the need to supply classroom teachers with materials on ethnic differences (e.g., classroom films on modern Japan)

(7) the need for the helping professional to serve as a sensitive and special support system as the child begins the adjustment process in the particular school setting

(8) the need for the helping professional to suggest environmental modifications for the Japanese child (e.g., tutors within the school setting or particular schools in the area that serve foreign-language children)

(9) the difficulties of the Japanese student and his or her family with the English language (referral of family to English-language courses)

(10) the need for the helping professional to assist the family in securing outside community resources

(11) the need of the Japanese student to continue learning the Japanese language

(12) the need of the family for information on customs of the dominant culture along with social and psychological support for themselves

(13) the need for Japanese-American cultural exchange enrichment programs so that members of both cultures can appreciate unique resources such as food, drama, dance, music, arts, and crafts (coordinate cultural exchange programs either in a classroom or for the whole school)

Keeping in mind the generational orientation of Japanese Americans (Issei, Nisei, or Sansei), and recognizing where they may be on a continuum as to degree of assimilation and acculturation, it is important to note that many Japanese Americans are still sometimes placed in situations of extreme cultural conflict.

Sue and Sue (1971) have devised three different categories with which Asian students may identify in order to deal with the conflicting demands of two cultures:

(1) *traditionalist:* individuals who remain "loyal" to their own ethnic group by retaining traditional values and living up to expectations of the family

(2) *marginal person:* individuals who attempt to become over-Westernized by rejecting traditional Asian values

(3) *yellow power person:* individual who is rebelling against parental authority as he or she attempts to develop a new identity that will enable a reconciliation of viable aspects of his or her heritage with the present situation

With clients of the traditionalist orientation, the counselor must be aware of intense feelings of guilt and shame present and the likelihood that psychological symptoms will be presented as psychophysiological reactions and vocational indecision. In this instance dominant-culture helpers will need to take a much more active approach to structuring the sessions (respect for authority) and must deal specifically with issues of confidentiality. Cultural racism and its effects on positive acculturation will be the issues to target with the marginal person. Due to the militancy of the yellow power person against the weaknesses of society, the counselor's aim here will be to help the client disentangle the racist society issues from personal problem issues. Obviously, since the counselor him- or herself will represent the establishment, rapport will be difficult to achieve (Sue & Sue, 1971).

Nishio's (1982, pp. 10-11) findings suggest that American clinicians and counselors take the following therapeutic and nontraditional approaches with Japanese-American clients:

(1) Give advice.
(2) Offer environmental and practical help.
(3) Make home visits and/or be available at irregular hours.
(4) Deal with the issue of the client's being of Japanese descent.
(5) Utilize Japanese modes of psychotherapy (e.g., Naikan therapy, Morita therapy).
(6) Provide education and consciousness-raising.
(7) Offer telephone sessions.
(8) Make collateral contacts (work with other professionals, agencies, and parents).
(9) Utilize cultural knowledge and experience.
(10) Participate in social dialogue before working on problems.

A group-centered approach that might be used by a educators and counselors is suggested by Kaneshige (1973):

(1) Provide a nonthreatening group climate to encourage more verbal participation.
(2) Verbalize to group members some of the cultural value differences.
(3) Minimize interruptions of other group members while the nonexpressive Asian is speaking.
(4) Assure confidentiality.
(5) Clarify and interpret the expressions of all group members.
(6) Challenge Caucasian-American critical statements to Asians.
(7) Recognize one's role as an authority figure to the Asian student.
(8) Encourage listening skills of other group members.
(9) Encourage the Asian-American student to change his or her pattern of behavior as an outcome of personal growth rather than as a statement of denying cultural identity.

As Callao (1973) as well as others have asserted, counselors working with Japanese-American or other Asian-American clients have a responsibility to be aware of their clients' life-styles, and not just the latest techniques and research methods. For instance, the concepts of shame and interpersonal relationships within the family may not only prevent Japanese Americans from utilizing services in the first place, but may be a motivating force that prevents those who do seek services from joining in the counseling process. Motet (1981) suggests that other factors to be aware of in the counseling process are misinterpretation of nonverbal cues, dominant-culture customs that are offensive to the Japanese, age and sex factors in terms of selection of the helper, and the slowness of rapport building.

Not only do educators and counselors working with Japanese-American clients have a responsibility to be aware of their clients' life-styles, but, further, they have a responsibility to function as change agents in existing institutions to foster a helping environment that can truly benefit Japanese Americans. Included in such service delivery would be changes in mental health policies (personnel as well as selection of techniques), establishment of community agencies designed to serve the needs of Asian persons (financial, career counseling, and networking for social and psychological support), educational reevaluation (encouraging creativity among Japanese-American students rather than stereotyping them as suited only for the physical sciences), and advocacy for more governmental intervention to assure Asians financial assistance for degrees in higher education.

Questions for Review and Reflection

(1) What impact did the concentration camp internment have on Japanese-American culture? Why should or should not this event be prominent in a discussion of Japanese Americans?

(2) How does the strong caste system culture of Japanese Americans influence their acculturation into the dominant culture?

(3) What factors contribute to Japanese Americans' being called a "model minority"? What danger, if any, exists in such a label? How does this label affect Japanese-American relationships with other Asian Americans?

(4) How does knowledge of the generation from which Japanese Americans come help in establishing educational or counseling goals for them? Identify a concern and describe how you might approach it based on the generation of the Japanese student or client.

(5) What Japanese-American values are responsible for the relative success of Japanese Americans in the dominant culture of the United States? Are these values different from those of the dominant culture, or are Japanese

Americans better at living according to the values than dominant culture members?

(6) How does the allegiance of Japanese Americans to family influence educational or counseling practices?

(7) How does the relationship between the governments of the United States and Japan affect Japanese Americans and their relationships with members of the dominant culture and other culturally different persons in the United States?

(8) What unique problems might one expect the Kibei to experience that are different from problems experienced by other Japanese Americans?

(9) What impact does traditional body language of Japanese Americans have on their interactions with members of the dominant culture? How can educators or counselors prevent miscommunication in these encounters?

(10) Henkin (1985) describes a unique form of prejudice directed at the Sansei. How can educators or counselors explore this prejudice from the perspective of both dominant-culture values and Japanese-American values?

References

Benedict, R. (1945). *The chrysanthemum and the sword: Patterns of Japanese culture.* New York: New American Library.

Callao, M. J. (1973). Culture shock: West, East, and West again. *Personnel and Guidance Journal, 51,* 413-416.

Chu, R. (1971). *Majors of Chinese and Japanese students at the University of California, Berkeley for the past 20 years* (Project Report, AS150, Asian Studies Division). Berkeley: University of California.

Chuman, F. F. (1976). *The bamboo people: The law and Japanese Americans.* Chicago: Japanese American Citizens League.

The drive to excel. (1984, April). *Newsweek on Campus.*

Garfinkle, P. (1983). The best "Jewish mother" in the world. *Psychology Today, 17,* 56-60.

Hansen, M. L. (1952). The problem of the third generation immigrant. *Commentary, 14,* 492-500.

Henkin, W. A. (1985). Toward counseling the Japanese in America: A cross-cultural primer. *Journal of Counseling and Development, 63,* 500-503.

Jenkins, D. (1973). *Job power: Blue and white collar democracy.* Garden City, NY: Doubleday.

Kagiwada, G., & Fujimote, I. (1973). Asian-American studies: Implications for education. *Personnel and Guidance Journal, 51,* 397-405.

Kaneshige, E. (1973). Cultural factors in group counseling and interaction. *Personnel and Guidance Journal, 51,* 407-412.

Kikumura, A., & Kitano, H. (1973). Interracial marriage: A picture of the Japanese Americans. *Journal of Social Issues, 29,* 67-81.

Kitano, H. H. L. (1976). *Japanese Americans.* Englewood Cliffs, NJ: Prentice-Hall.

Kurokawa, N. (1968). Lineal orientation in child rearing among Japanese. *Journal of Marriage and Family, 30,* 129-135.

Masuda, M., Matsumoto, G. H., & Meredith, G. (1970). Ethnic identity in three generations of Japanese-Americans. *Journal of Social Psychology, 81,* 199-207.

Montero, D. (1981). The Japanese Americans: Changing patterns of assimilation over three generations. *American Sociological Review, 46,* 829-839.

Motet, D. (1981, April 9-12). *Adjustment therapy with Japanese.* Paper presented at the annual meeting of the Western Psychological Association, Los Angeles.

Nakane, C. (1972). *Human relations in Japan.* Tokyo: Ministry of Foreign Affairs.

Nishio, K. (1982, August 23-27). *Characteristics of Japanese and Americans in psychotherapy in Japan and the United States.* Paper presented at the annual meeting of the American Psychological Association, Washington, DC.

Okihiro, G. Y., & Sly, J. (1983). The press, Japanese Americans, and the concentration camps. *Phylon, 44,* 66-83.

Padilla, A. M., Wagatsuma, Y., & Lindholm, K. J. (1985). Acculturation and personality as predictors of stress in Japanese and Japanese Americans. *Journal of Social Psychology, 125,* 295-305.

Petersen, W. (1971). *Japanese Americans.* New York: Random House.

Powell, B., & Martin, B. (1988, February 4). The Pacific century. *Newsweek,* pp. 42-58.

Ravich, R., & Wyden, B. (1974). *Predictable pairing.* New York: Wyden.

Smith, R. J., & Beardsley, R. K. (1962). *Japanese culture: Its development and characteristics.* Chicago: Aldine.

Success story: Outwitting the whites. (1971, June). *Newsweek.*

Sue, D. W. (1981). *Counseling the culturally different: Theory and practice.* New York: John Wiley.

Sue, D. W., & Kirk, B. (1972). Psychological characteristics of Chinese American students. *Journal of Counseling Psychology, 2,* 11-17.

Sue, D. W., & Sue, D. (1973). Understanding Asian Americans: The neglected minority. *Personnel and Guidance Journal, 51,* 385-389.

Sue, D. W., & Sue, D. (1990). *Counseling the culturally different: Theory and practice* (2nd ed.). New York: John Wiley.

Sue, S., & Sue, D. W. (1971). Chinese-American personality and mental health. *Amerasia Journal, 1,* 36-49.

Tinker, J. (1973). Intermarriage and ethnic boundaries: The Japanese American case. *Journal of Social Issues, 29,* 49-66.

Tomine, S. I. (1991). Counseling Japanese Americans: From internment to reparation. In C. C. Lee & B. L. Richardson (Eds.), *Multicultural issues in counseling: New approaches to diversity* (pp. 91-105). Alexandria, VA: American Association for Counseling and Development.

Watanabe, C. (1973). Self-expression and the Asian-American experience. *Personnel and Guidance Journal, 51,* 390-396.

Wilson, R. A., & Hosokawa, B. (1980). *East to America: A history of the Japanese in the United States.* New York: William Morrow.

6

Chinese Americans

The first Chinese came to the United States in search of wealth. California offered a chance to those who could not succeed in their home country and who were able to find passage across the Pacific. The Chinese who came to the United States were viewed by other Americans as a mass of contradictions. They were seen as "clean" because of personal appearance, yet "filthy" because they lived in cramped living quarters. They were viewed as "thrifty" because they spent little on food or clothing, yet "extravagant" because of the money they put into traditional feasts. They were labeled as "bright" because they learned quickly and succeeded in several industries, yet "stupid" because they would not adopt American customs. They were treated with both admiration and curiosity. Clearly, the Chinese were judged by standards other than their own.

This immigration of Chinese to the United States began about 1840. As Sue (1981) has noted, the Chinese were the first Asian group to arrive in the United States in large numbers. The discovery of gold in California served as a magnet, drawing the people of southern China and those of the eastern United States together in Sacramento Valley. There was a high demand for cheap labor to build the transcontinental railroad because the gold seekers had no intention of performing those menial tasks. It was under those circumstances that the Chinese were sought. The demand for laborers, coupled with political unrest and overpopulation in certain provinces in

China, brought a steady stream of Chinese to the United States. By the 1860s, nearly all the Chinese immigrants had settled on the West Coast, with the heaviest concentrations in California.

When the Chinese first arrived in California their presence filled a void in the labor market. However, a series of business recessions, coupled with the completion of the Union Pacific Railroad in 1869, made competition for jobs fierce. When working men began to see the Chinese as an economic threat, labor organizations began to agitate against them.

Oppression of the Chinese began in the mining districts. A law was passed (later declared unconstitutional) that taxed the Chinese miners. In 1852 the Miner's Convention banned all Chinese, and hatred of the Chinese grew in cities and mining camps. Since the Chinese rarely defended themselves, they became easy targets for the rowdy miners. They were robbed, beaten, and tortured, often for no reason at all (Wood, 1974).

In San Francisco, where large numbers of Chinese lived, the police and the courts were quite severe in arresting and sentencing Chinese for crimes such as gambling, prostitution, theft, and disturbing the peace. Fines and jail sentences were usually stiff, and not comparable to those imposed on non-Chinese defendants. Ordinances were passed that were aimed directly at the Chinese, such as those requiring laundries to be constructed with stone or brick walls and the Cubic Air Ordinance, which required that every lodging house provide at least 500 cubic feet of air space for every lodger. Eventually, the great rise of anti-Chinese sentiment resulted in the first U.S. law restricting the immigration of an entire race of people. The Chinese Exclusion Act of 1882 was not repealed until 1943 (Sandmeyer, 1973).

Acculturation

The Chinese, like others, have found that coexistence of their culture with the dominant culture of the United States has created problems that they otherwise would not encounter. The process of acculturation takes place on two levels—externally and internally. External acculturation is behavioral—individuals acquire the material trappings, common language, and secular roles of the dominant culture. Internal acculturation involves the acquisition of the dominant cultures attitudes (Zanden, 1983).

The first Chinese to arrive in the United States found themselves in a new land among new people with new ways. To ease their fears and sense of loneliness and to find comfort in the familiar, the Chinese clung together. They ate their own food, wore the clothing they were accustomed to wearing in China, and followed their own customs and traditions. When they settled in the United States they brought with them ideas, customs, institutions, and practices that became the bases for the communities they established, known as Chinatowns.

Despite more than a century of migration, the Chinese have not fully adopted the culture, language, and behavior of the United States. While no people from outside cultures seem ever to have been fully absorbed by a host culture, the forms and techniques by which the Chinese have maintained their traditions are unique. Their cultural and social exclusivity within the cities of the host cultures is a phenomenon of worldwide historical significance.

Like any other group, the Chinese in the United States are not all alike; different segments of the Chinese-American population have different attitudes toward the mainstream culture. The *Lo Wah Kiu* (older immigrants who came to the United States before 1965) cling to the Chinese mode of living, and many are convinced that they will never be treated equally by the dominant culture. They live in Chinatowns in larger cities, read only Chinese newspapers, listen to Chinese music, eat Chinese foods, and socialize only with other Chinese. These old immigrants (some of whom are successful entrepreneurs) also stay in Chinatowns for economic and political reasons, as they can find cheap labor there and have more influence within their own ethnic neighborhoods (Wong, 1982).

Native-born Chinese Americans and foreign-born Chinese who are citizens of the United States (*Wa Yeoy*) constitute a solid professional group with similar aspirations. They tend to desire total acceptance by the dominant culture and are willing to fight for equal treatment. They often work as professionals. Interracial marriage is high among this group. These Chinese Americans work hard to bring more social agencies and community organizations to the various Chinatowns.

The term *new immigrants* refers to the group of Chinese Americans who settled after 1965. They tend to be more educated than the old immigrants and to come from urban areas of China. Their primary goal in coming to the United States is economic betterment. These new immigrants aim to transmit their cultural heritage to their children as well as to blend in certain aspects of the dominant culture of the United States.

Within the Chinese-American culture is also a group of disenchanted youth who have been recruited as "muscle men" for the Chinese gambling rooms. These youth gangs practice Chinese martial arts and flaunt their "ethnic chauvinism" when confronted by other ethnic gangs (Wong, 1982).

It should be noted that many Chinese immigrants to the United States had no intention of remaining here, and this is the reason they held on to their own culture. In their traditional culture, the set of mores defines a strong obligation of the individual to the family and to those of superior class. These obligations include group loyalty and obedience; avoidance of embarrassing situations; modesty, humility, and respect in the presence of superiors; and the absence of complaining in the face of hardship. Because they created their own communities they were able to retain these cultural values. By forming their own communities and exhibiting nonthreatening qualities, they were able to resist acculturation without arousing the concern of the dominant group.

Poverty and Economic Concerns

In contrast to many other cultural groups, Chinese Americans have a contemporary image as a highly successful minority that has made it economically. Sue (1981) reports that the general perception is that Chinese Americans have exceeded the national median income and that they complete a higher median number of grades in school than do members of other cultural groups. However, it needs to be taken into account that Asian families often have more than one wage earner. Also, although Asian wage earners may have higher levels of education, their wages are not commensurate with their training.

Owing to laws not changed until as late as 1940, some states that forbade Chinese to go into many occupations (e.g., dentist, chauffeur, pilot, architect, teacher) carved out an economic niche for the Chinese Americans. They became laundry operators and restaurateurs; they opened garment factories, novelty shops, and grocery stores. Because many jobs demand a good command of Standard English, Chinese Americans have often been excluded. As of the 1970 census, of 432,000 Chinese Americans, 40% were professionals, technical workers, and administrators, and the rest were in other types of businesses (Wong, 1982).

Kinship plays a decisive role in the activities of many Chinese businesspersons. To start a small-scale family firm is the dream of many Chinese immigrants. Independence, profit, and being in control of one's employment are aspirations of many Chinese Americans. By accumulating capital from many years of hard work and pooling all the savings from all family members, quite a few small-scale businesses have been started. All family members who are able usually work in the family firm, but major decisions are typically made by the head of the family. Family members are expected to work harder than outsiders and are often underpaid because it is the family's business. Thus low pay, hard work, and long hours are part of the economic reality for many Chinese Americans (Wong, 1982).

History of Oppression

The Chinese were subject to oppression even before they arrived in the United States. American interest in China dates from the time of colonial commerce with Canton. Interest in Chinese material culture was not matched by a sympathy for the Chinese people, however. According to Miller (1969), American traders in China reported that the Chinese were "ridiculously clad, superstitious ridden, dishonest, crafty, cruel, and marginal members of the human race who lacked the courage, intelligence, skill, and will to do anything about the oppressive despotism under which they lived or the stagnating social conditions that surrounded them" (p. 36).

Although trader prejudices were limited for the most part to commentaries arising out of experiences with Chinese merchants, American Protestant missionaries, ruled by passion for their divine mission, tended to impugn the morality of the whole Chinese nation. To missionaries bent on conversion, the ordinary Chinese were debased heathens awaiting divine rescue from their unholy condition of "lechery, dishonesty, cruelty, filth, and intellectual inferiority" (Miller, 1969, p. 37). Thus by the time Chinese made their appearance in the United States they had been preceded by an almost entirely negative stereotype.

Although a national feeling against the Chinese had been aroused even before the first immigrants arrived, it was their presence in California mines and in other primary labor forces and the prediction that they would flood the whole country that triggered oppressive action.

A series of business setbacks and the completion of the Union Central Pacific Railroad in 1869 made jobs scarce. Because the Chinese represented a large percentage of the work force, the white workers began to see them as an economic threat. Thus much of the Chinese oppression from the dominant group emerged when the market fell through in Comstock Lode mining stocks in 1876 and a depression resulted. Many were affected by this depression, and discontent and unrest were widespread. It was in this setting that whites looked for a scapegoat, and the presence of the Chinese changed from a blessing to a curse (McClellan, 1971).

The Chinese, with their different dress, clannish ways, pigtails, and docile manner, were a perfect target. It was of no consequence that the jobs filled by the Chinese were scorned by white men when white laborers started rallying against the Chinese. Daniels (1971) notes that "the movement soon developed an ideology of white supremacy and Oriental inferiority that was wholly compatible with the mainstream of American racism" (p. 43).

Language and the Arts

The values embodied in traditional Chinese painting are those of the Confucian scholar or Taoist recluse—searching for truth in nature. Nature is seen by the Chinese as a partner in a harmonious productive relationship with humankind. This attitude has permeated Chinese culture and art over the centuries. China has the world's longest continuous cultural history, and the last 8,000 have left an abundance of paintings, calligraphy, sculptures, ceramics, jades, bronzes, tombs, gardens, and architecture. Many of these treasures pay homage to the long and varied history of religion in China, the folk spirits, the tranquil Taoist contemplation of nature, and the monumental Buddhist cave temples (Juliano, 1981).

For thousands of years the Chinese have been obsessed with the links between generations—past, present, and future. Ancestor worship is a major part of Chinese culture, stimulating art and ritual. Reverence for the past is evidenced in the enormous energies devoted to tombs, rituals, and burial customs.

Because the Chinese still use the past as a standard by which to gauge the present, the subjects and purposes of most ancient and modern art have a great deal in common. Whether the art is Confucian (social) or Taoist (individualistic), a moral philosophical or religious message is behind every painting. Unlike many Western artists, the Chinese artist does not attempt to depict exactly what is seen, but rather to capture the essence (or essential nature) of the subject. Hence Chinese art is characterized by a lack of realism. Instead, Chinese art reaffirms a personal harmonious relationship with nature in providing a "visible manifestation of the life-giving spirit that animates nature" (Terrill, 1979, p. 309).

Another important factor binding the present to the past is the Chinese language itself. Written language is neither alphabetic nor phonetic; it is independent of sound, evolving separately from the spoken language and much more slowly. The ideograms composing the Chinese script were standardized very early in 221 B.C. (Han Dynasty) and helped unite China as a nation. Nearly frozen in time, the written language has been an enormously conservative force in the culture. As pictures of ideas, Chinese characters travel directly from the eye to the brain, bypassing pathways of speech. Westerners who never quite mastered spelling and who respond to pictures will find themselves drawn to written Chinese. The best tool for writing the language is a brush, which creates an individual work of art with each letter (Juliano, 1981).

Because the Chinese language has a different symbol for each word (about 25,000 Chinese characters exist), the written language is hard to learn. Chinese children must study much longer than their American counterparts. As Chang and Chang (1978) have put it, "Dictionaries and telephone books are clumsy servants" when written in Chinese (p. 13).

While written Chinese is standardized and is read by educated Chinese throughout the world, the spoken language is extremely varied. There are many Chinese dialects, and they can be as different from each other as English is from German. It is not uncommon for a single family, separated by civil strife, to share several different dialects.

The heavy emphasis on language memorization is partially responsible for the selection of applied and natural sciences as majors for many Chinese students in the United States. Well-developed memorization skills are part of the reason many Chinese students excel in the sciences. Science and math courses also require less English fluency than courses in the humanities and social sciences. This contributes to Chinese Americans' electing to take these courses.

Racism and Prejudice

The Chinese, easily identifiable racially and culturally, became the unwilling victims of derogatory stereotyping in the United States. In addition to racial and cultural distinctiveness, the mutually reinforcing factors of spatial and social isolation provided ingredients for discrimination and prejudice. Laws were passed forbidding Chinese from owning property, voting, or testifying against white people (Lyman, 1974).

Kagiwada and Fujimoto (1973) point out that the first Chinese coming to this country found conditions little better than slavery. The first immigrants were all males, since the only females allowed to immigrate were prostitutes. Chinese men were prohibited from marrying white women. The phrase "not a Chinaman's chance" describes the conditions faced by these early Chinese immigrants. The pervasive attitude of the dominant culture culminated in the passage of the Chinese Exclusion Act of 1882, the only federal statute to deny citizenship to an entire people because they were considered undesirable.

Sue and Sue (1973) characterize the success myth concerning Asian immigrants as a continuation of racist and prejudicial thinking. The myth holds that Chinese are not experiencing adjustment problems, but have been successful in the dominant culture. This kind of faulty thinking suggests that in this culture individuals can succeed if they work hard enough. Therefore, if one does not succeed it is not because of forces operating in society, but because of other factors such as racial inferiority or inappropriate values. A close examination of the plight of Chinese Americans does not support the success myth. While many Chinese have obtained high educational status, there is still evidence of racism practiced against Chinese Americans.

Sociopolitical Factors

In the home communities of Chinese Americans, kinship relations were used to organize social and economic life. Many villages consisted of single lineages, which were patrilineal and exogamous. The group shared a common ancestor associated with a locality. The males were members of the lineage, and women joined their husbands' lineage through marriage. In the United States, Chinese may or may not share common blood or locality ties, but they often group together under common surnames such as Lee or Chan. This practice arose from the needs of early immigrants, many of whom were married adult males who had left their wives behind in China and thus lacked family life.

Within the family name associations are smaller groups called *fongs* that share both a common surname and common village of origin. The fongs and family name associations perform functions similar to those in the homeland—social, ritual, dispute settlement, and welfare. Some surname groups were small, so they united with other groups according to traditional family alliances to form larger multifamily name associations according to neighboring home districts in China.

Next to family and kinship, common geographic origin provides an important basis for voluntary associations in traditional China. In the United States, Chinese have used this idea to form regional organizations. These district associations act as credit clubs and have their own credit unions. They also elect officials for Spring and Autumn Sacrifices. In order to get elected, candidates donate thousands of dollars to community activities. The elected leaders enjoy prestige in the business community and will often be invited to join in economic partnerships and other gainful pursuits (Wong, 1982).

Because of attacks by members of the dominant culture on Chinese businesses, since 1933 Chinese business owners have regularly formed trade associations, such as the American-Chinese Restaurant Association and the Chinese Chamber of Commerce. These associations often negotiate with the larger culture on matters of Chinese business. They provide information on taxes, sanitation, wages, and licenses, and advise members about technical and legal details. They donate to cultural activities and to improving resources in the community.

In the early days of the family associations and district associations, merchants easily assumed positions of dominance due to their positions as brokers who extended credit and negotiated employment for peasants seeking passage to the United States. Later these merchants received additional status by assuming positions as spokesmen who represented Chinatown communities on the outside.

Resentment against merchant domination of early Chinese society, coupled with the anti-Chinese climate in the late nineteenth and early twentieth centuries in the United States, contributed to the formation of *tongs*. Tongs were patterned after secret societies in China and attracted discontented elements of society. In most cases, they were formed to deal with some local situation of oppression. The tongs were also involved in gambling and prostitution, and financed youth gangs to police streets and protect gambling dens (Nee, 1974).

Child-Rearing Practices

Relationships between parents and children are based on the dual principles of filial piety and veneration of age. Filial piety demands absolute obedience and complete devotion to the parents. This is enhanced by genuine affection between parents and children and emotional bonds of mutual interdependence. Children depend on their parents when young; parents depend on their sons for security in old age.

Chinese children tend to be very well behaved, especially in public. Parents use a combination of gentle admonition and encouragement for discipline and would consider it a loss of face if they had to become angry in public (Sidel, 1972). The primary means by which parents keep family members in line is through the use of guilt, shame, and appeals to obligation. Shame is the most powerful of these for motivating children, because it provides a frame of reference by connecting the child to other Chinese. Guilt, on the other hand, is a highly individualistic concept. If children attempt to act independently of their parents wishes, they are labeled selfish, inconsiderate, and ungrateful (Sue, 1981).

Religious Practices

The religious roots of the Chinese are varied. The scholar gentry class practiced Confucianism, which is considered more a philosophy than a religion. Confucianism is directed toward solving the practical concerns of everyday life: social relationships, government, and ethical concerns. It teaches respect for education and encourages education throughout one's life. Heaven is thought of as a universal moral law, a cosmic order. Just as nature should move in accord with this ultimate law, so should people. If they do, good things will happen to them. Unlike in Western religions, there is no sense of sin in Confucianism. Human nature is basically good and the evils of human society are due to the examples of immoral leaders. Morality does not rest on religious faith. Having no religious authority, the Chinese used the behaviors of good and wise men from the past as the chief source of values (Terrill, 1979).

In traditional Chinese thinking, the family was the center of society, so if China was to be a moral society, living in harmony with heaven's way, the place to begin was in family relationships. A hierarchical, class-stratified society was created in which each person knew his or her role and was expected to accept the inequalities of the system for the larger good. Sacrifices were offered to one's ancestors because it was believed that the spirits of the ancestors would punish moral offenders and see that good behavior was rewarded. Belief in life after death was also strengthened by the building of altars to one's ancestors and the placing of spirit tablets on them (Orr, 1980).

While the scholars embraced the intellectual aspects of Confucianism, the common people developed a folk religion that was supplemented over the centuries by the two other major Chinese religions, Buddhism and Taoism. Orr (1980) reports that very few Chinese, educated or not, found any great difficulty in following all of these religious traditions. Each was regarded as "a different road to the same destination" (p. 86). Folk religion assumes that the world is alive with spirits and gods, such as kitchen gods and earth gods. These deities have magical power and are feared. Many local gods were later interwoven with the gods of Buddhism and Taoism. Folk religion was closely tied to festivals such as New Year's, when family members returned to their ancestral villages. A wide variety of practices, such as divination, astrology, reading of palms, and dream interpretation, were used to determine what the gods intended and how to influence the unseen forces that controlled human life.

Taoism, another important Chinese religion, developed out of the life and writings of Lao-tzu. The central concept is that great inner peace and power come to persons who can center their lives on the way of the universe, or the *dao*. Through contemplation of nature, one's deepest and most human part can surface from the artificial expectations of society. Taoist priests used a variety of elixirs to delay or prevent death, taught breath control and exercises similar to Hatha yoga, and produced herbal medicines to heal and prolong life that are still used in traditional Chinese medicine.

Buddhism was established in China by missionary monks from Central Asia and was adapted to the Chinese culture. One of the great desires of the Chinese was assurance of life after death. Buddhism, with its teaching of reincarnation, was attractive to the Chinese. The most popular form of Buddhism became the Pure Land Sect, which held that all people were capable of salvation in one life if they achieved devotion to the Buddha through meritorious deeds and faith, kindness, and compassion (Orr, 1980).

The varied religious traditions among Chinese Americans are celebrated in festivals such as the Chinese New Year, "Sweeping of the Grave Festivals" dedicated to remembering the dead, and the Mid-Autumn Festival, which is rooted in many ancient legends and celebrates fertility and longevity (Wong, 1982). Although the Chinese have mingled some of the ideas of Christianity with their own religions, most Chinese people have not converted to Christianity (Bonavia, 1980).

Family Structure and Dynamics

In the traditional Chinese family, age, sex, and generational status are the primary determinants of role behavior. Ancestors and elders are viewed with great reverence and respect. The father is the head of the household, and his authority is unquestioned. The primary duty of the male is to be a good son, and obligations to be a good husband or a good father are secondary. For this reason, the primary allegiance of a son is to the family into which he is born. Females are subservient to males and perform all domestic duties, although in many Chinese-American families, both the husband and wife work outside the home, often in the family business (Sue, 1981).

Traditionally, females in China were not treated the same as males. In ancient times, many female babies were drowned at birth; if they survived to between the ages of 5 and 7, they might have their feet bound tightly, so that, in the future, walking would be difficult. Women were denied an education and discouraged from developing any skills outside of those related to the home (Sidel, 1972). Marriages were arranged, and young brides, who were considered to belong to their husbands' families, were discouraged from even visiting their own families. Wives were particularly subservient to their mothers-in-law. This subservient role would be rectified somewhat later in life when a woman had a chance to dominate the wives of her own sons.

In Chinese-American culture, a subtle and indirect approach to problems is valued over an open and straightforward one; the avoidance of offending others is emphasized. Family members are encouraged to restrain feelings that may disrupt family harmony. Since there is much homogeneity in the culture, much of the communication is contextually determined, leaving little need to be verbally confrontational. Dependence, conformity, and restraint of disruptive emotions are valued in the development of character.

The welfare and integrity of the family is of the utmost importance. Individual family members are expected to put the welfare of the family and its reputation before their own individual needs. The behavior of each family member is considered to reflect on the entire family. Therefore there is much cultural pressure to behave in a manner that will not embarrass or shame one's family and cause them to "lose face." So important is the reputation of the family that problems such as failure in school or juvenile delinquency are handled as much as possible within the family, and public admission of these problems is suppressed (Sue, 1981). When irreconcilable problems do arise, face is restored by formally disowning the child.

Because of the cultural pressure to maintain family integrity and because Chinese youth identify more with their families than with their peers, sexual intercourse before marriage is not common. Illegitimacy, abortion, and divorce are also rare (Sidel, 1972).

Cultural Values and Attitudes

Chinese values are reflected in all aspects of the Chinese life-style. Selflessness is one of the oldest values in China. The selfless person is always willing to subordinate his or her own interest or the interest of a small group to the interest of a larger social group. This grew out of the beliefs of the Confucians, who perceived the individual as part of a network of related social positions. Obedience to authority is taken as a sign of selflessness, since the leaders of an organization are understood to be working on behalf of the interests of the whole. This value of selflessness, or deference to the collective unit, is quite different from the value of individualism and individual rights of the dominant culture of the United States.

A second contemporary value rooted in Confucianism is "knowing the meaning of your work" and understanding the interrelatedness of tasks (doing versus being). This involves understanding how subordinate tasks are related to a greater goal and is instrumental in fostering the cheerful approach of the Chinese toward all kinds of work.

Harmony, or the avoidance of conflict, especially in the area of social relations, is valued in the Chinese culture. The ideal of harmony also applies to the relationship between people and nature and to a person's inner psyche, for which breath control and meditation are employed to help foster tranquility.

Another value is related to the concept of peer respect and the avoidance of disrespect to enforce compliance with rules or to motivate toward education. One interesting practice in many rural Chinese villages is for the entire village to laugh at someone who has violated a social norm. This method of societal control over its members contrasts sharply with the fear of arrest and punishment used in the United States (Terrill, 1979).

Many Chinese Americans still hold to cultural values and attitudes that are deeply rooted in their native culture. With the process of acculturation, many Chinese Americans have adapted while maintaining such traditional values as belief in the family structure, an emphasis on education, and a strong system of discipline.

Implications

Chinese Americans migrated to this country to escape difficult political, economic, and social conditions. Initially, the Chinese were welcomed in the western United States as a source of cheap labor. But as the United States moved into the post-Civil War period, American labor began feeling the competitive economic pinch. Out of a situation involving competition for jobs and high social visibility, there arose the cry "The Chinese must go." The Chinese were severely persecuted, subjected to threats and violence. Some responded by dispersing throughout the country and settling in Chinatowns within urban areas. In the Chinatowns they could maintain their cultural identity and advance themselves economically through hard work, sacrifice, and education. Most of them intended to return to China after they attained their economic goals, but the anti-Chinese agitation in the late 1870s, coupled with lack of income, deferred that dream.

The traditional Chinese way enabled Chinese Americans to survive in the United States as well as to develop economic stability. In spite of vicious racism and discrimination, the Chinese survived the attempt to be acculturated by the dominant culture. Still among Chinese Americans a strong value of kinship loyalty exists. Such values should not be eradicated, but rather should be respected and appreciated.

In order to counsel or teach Chinese Americans effectively, the helping professional must create a relationship between cultures by simultaneously understanding his or her own culture and that of the client or student. Helpers must first be aware of their own cultural heritages and worldviews before they will be able to understand and appreciate those of the culturally diverse individuals they serve. Counseling and education curricula should include opportunities for clients and students to explore such issues with counselors and teachers.

Chinese Americans appear to be more acculturated than other groups. However, this may be because of their own cultural tendencies to conform, obey authority, and restrain strong feelings. Furthermore, family honor is so important to many Chinese Americans that they suppress any admission of personal problems. For this reason, Chinese Americans may first present personal problems in the form of physical or vocational complaints. Counselors must initially respond to these "superficial" problems in an effort to establish a relationship of trust (Sue, 1981; Sue & Sue, 1990).

An educator working with a Chinese American must first determine whether he or she is traditional, acculturated, marginal, or bicultural, since interactions with the dominant culture will often hinge on the Chinese American's view of his or her own culture. For example, if a Chinese American is traditional, the educator needs to offer a logical, rational, structured approach over an affective, reflective, ambiguous one. If the Chinese American is marginal, he or she must be helped to distinguish between negative rejection of his or her own culture and positive attempts to acculturate. This process requires a great deal of cultural knowledge and flexibility with regard to both theory and technique on the part of the educator (Sue, 1981; Sue & Sue, 1990).

It is only through an awareness and acceptance of all aspects of the Chinese-American culture that educators can truly understand the complexity of human behaviors of Chinese Americans. Chinese Americans continue to be both Chinese and American, and they must be able to do so without sacrificing the security their ethnic identity provides or the challenge offered by the dominant culture.

Questions for Review and Reflection

(1) What differences in degree of acculturation are likely to exist between the Lo Wah Kiu and the Wa Yeoy? How can educators and counselors use the knowledge of these differences in working with Chinese Americans?

(2) How does the Chinese view of nature influence Chinese-American interactions with other people?

(3) What impact does the Chinese reverence for the past have on Chinese Americans?

(4) What factors appear to be primarily responsible for Chinese-American success in science and engineering? How can educators or counselors determine if a Chinese-American student should be directed toward science or engineering or to some other career path?

(5) What is meant by the phrase "not a Chinaman's chance"? In what ways do you think the use of the phrase influences Chinese-American interactions with the dominant culture?

(6) What misperceptions exist within the success myth associated with Chinese Americans?

(7) What are fongs? What is the role of family and kinship in business and economic concerns for Chinese Americans?

(8) How can educators or counselors help Chinese-American children develop positive self-esteem when Chinese parents use guilt and shame in the discipline of their children?

(9) How can educators or counselors work with traditional Chinese-American females whose culture prescribes a different role from female assertiveness found in the dominant culture?

(10) What impact does the traditionally subtle and indirect approach to problems used by Chinese Americans have in a dominant culture that values a more open, direct, and honest approach?

References

Bonavia, D. (1980). *The Chinese*. New York: Lippincott & Crowell.

Chang, R., & Chang, M. S. (1978). *Speaking of Chinese*. New York: W. W. Norton.

Daniels, R. (1971). *Concentration camps USA: Japanese Americans and World War II*. New York: Holt, Rinehart & Winston.

Juliano, A. (1981). *Treasures of China*. New York: Richard Marek.

Kagiwada, G., & Fujimoto, I. (1973). Asian-American studies: Implications for education. *Personnel and Guidance Journal, 51*, 400-405.

Lyman, S. M. (1974). *Chinese Americans*. New York: Random House.

McClellan, R. (1971). *The heathen Chinese*. Athens: Ohio University Press.

Miller, S. C. (1969). *The unwelcome immigrant: The American image of the Chinese, 1785-1882.* Los Angeles: University of California Press.

Nee, B. D. (1974). *Longtime Californian: A documentary study of an American Chinatown.* Boston: Houghton Mifflin.

Orr, R. G. (1980). *Religion in China.* New York: Friendship.

Sandmeyer, E. C. (1973). *The anti-Chinese movement in California.* Urbana: University of Illinois Press.

Sidel, R. (1972). *Women and child care in China.* New York: Hill & Wang.

Sue, D. W. (1981). *Counseling the culturally different: Theory and practice.* New York: John Wiley.

Sue, D. W., & Sue, D. (1973). Asian-Americans: The neglected minority. *Personnel and Guidance Journal, 51,* 386-389.

Sue, D. W., & Sue, D. (1990). *Counseling the culturally different: Theory and practice* (2nd ed.). New York: John Wiley.

Terrill, R. (Ed.). (1979). *The China difference.* New York: Harper & Row.

Wong, B. P. (1982). *Chinatown: Economic adaptation and ethnic identity of the Chinese.* New York: Holt, Rinehart & Winston.

Wood, E. R. (1974). *Californians and Chinese: The first decade.* San Francisco: R&E Research Associates.

Zanden, J. W. (1983). *American minority relations.* New York: Knopf.

7

Vietnamese in the United States

An initial, naive thought about Vietnamese people who immigrated to the United States could lead to the question of why these people came. Lee and Rong (1988) report that the Vietnamese population in the United States was approximately 245,000 (of whom 90% were born in Vietnam) in 1980; they project an increase to 1.6 million by the year 2000. The total Southeast Asian refugee population in the United States was 711,000 in September 1984 (Office of Refugee Resettlement, 1985). The American press in the 1970s would have had readers believe that U.S. troops were none too politely asked to leave Vietnam because the entire North and South Vietnamese populations desired communist domination. Our political leaders astutely pursued withdrawal at the appropriate time, thus avoiding further loss of American life and unfair treatment at the hands of communism-loving Vietnamese while complying with the wishes of the people we had helped for so long.

Acceptance of such statements as truth would lead to the assumption that the Vietnamese who chose to follow the American troops to this free nation should have openly and willingly accepted acculturation into the dominant culture of the United States with few problems, little suffering, and grateful feelings toward their new country for taking them in. Since most Vietnamese had joined the communists, those few who came to the United States must have made a deliberate, well-thought-out decision to immigrate.

This idea, however, is not supported by the facts. Research has shown that the Vietnamese who fled their country were taking a path toward which they were driven by a total loss of personal and political freedom, economic deprivation, and a desperate need to survive the chaos in Vietnam.

Vietnam has been mightily affected by global influences throughout its history. Prior to French occupation in the mid-eighteenth century, the tribes of Viets were pursued and slaughtered by other Asians. The Chinese first invaded and tried to absorb the Lac-Viets, ancestors of today's Vietnamese, thousands of years ago. The Lac-Viets were encouraged by their leaders to fight for freedom from oppression and for maintenance of their separate cultural identity.

Resistance to colonization by France was occasionally vigorous and sometimes sporadic until World War I. The Vietnamese continued to resist and rebel against French rule, but some degree of order and stability was achieved at that time. World War II saw the Japanese arrive as conquerors, and resistance groups again arose. After the war and Japanese withdrawal, the French tried to regain control. The Chinese and British were also attempting to gain control of Vietnam, and the United States was becoming involved as well.

Modern-day bids for independence in Vietnam died with the Geneva Agreement, which called for a split in the country. The North was to be ruled by the communist regime under Ho Chi Minh; the South was to be governed by a system based on Western democracy. It appears that the Vietnamese people have been seeking freedom from global oppression throughout their entire history and over many centuries.

Acculturation

Basically, four groups of refugees came out of Vietnam: the first wave (1975), the second wave (1978-1979), the escapees ("boat people"), and those who left as a result of the 1979 Memorandum of Understanding between Vietnam and the United Nations High Commission for Refugees (the "orderly departure" program) (Haines, 1985). It is necessary to distinguish among these groups, because some researchers have found significant differences in the acculturation process among Vietnamese refugees based on how and when they came to the United States (S. Nguyen, 1982).

When the U.S. troops withdrew from Vietnam in 1975, approximately 135,000 Vietnamese left with them (Hawthorne, 1982). This massive withdrawal was preceded by several years of slow and deliberate abandonment of South Vietnam by the United States. When North Vietnam took over South Vietnam in 1975, the South Vietnamese people were astonished by a trail of broken promises and an end to aid and support by the United States. North Vietnam tightened its grip and imposed its totalitarian government on the South. Individual rights and liberties were suppressed, millions of people were jailed or sent to concentration camps without trial, and nearly the entire population was impoverished. The only alternative to imprisonment, death, and destruction of their homes for the South Vietnamese was an abrupt evacuation. They were called refugees, as distinguished from other migrants, because in the vast majority of cases they did not wish to leave Vietnam (Montero, 1979). Nguyen-Hong-Nhiem and Halpern (1989) describe the Vietnamese refugees who fled in 1975 as representing "the urban professional, business, managerial and government elites" (p. 11). Their acculturation has been described as easier and more successful than that of many subsequent immigrants from Vietnam, especially the boat people, who were sometimes of provincial working-class or rural peasant backgrounds.

After Vietnam was united under Hanoi's rule in 1976, conditions in South Vietnam became even more intolerable and appalling. More waves of refugees fled South Vietnam to be met in the United States by significant cultural difficulties: The language barrier created overwhelming problems in all attempts to acculturate; the Vietnamese people were denied the support of ethnically, culturally similar communities because they were dispersed in small groups across the country; and extended family units had been separated in their flight from Vietnam (Montero, 1979). Other factors that have an impact on the issue of acculturation include the escape process, survivor's guilt, and disillusionment with life in the United States.

The Vietnamese boat people escaped a country that had stabilized, but with a perceived level of oppression. Nguyen-Hong-Nhiem and Halpern (1989) describe the experience of these people:

> For those who survived the trip, safe landing and subsequent arrival at a refugee camp ended the second phase of the personal epic that began with the initial uprooting. Then followed the next stage, the long struggle for a return to "normalcy," with migration to a permanent home, a new norm, a new status, one that can never be equivalent to the old one, but one that does represent the reestablishment and renewal of self in a new sociocultural framework. (p. 10)

Cravens and Bornemann (1990) describe a fifth group of Vietnamese in the United States. They report that in fiscal year 1989, 8,721 Amerasians and immediate relatives of earlier Vietnamese refugees arrived in the United States. While these people were technically not refugees, the Amerasian Homecoming Act of 1987 provided the Amerasians all of the federal benefits afforded to refugees, including federal reimbursement to states that were willing to take in refugees. According to Cravens and Bornemann, "although quite diverse, the Amerasians can be described, when compared with their

Vietnamese peers, as having fewer years of formal education, fewer skills, and higher levels of general psychological distress" (p. 48). The Vietnamese acculturation was to be slow and extremely difficult. Many who fled were suspected of having psychological difficulties because of their having been noncommunists in a communist-dominated regime in Vietnam (Hawthorne, 1982). Another common dilemma for refugees in general faced Vietnamese refugees also. Refugees often have a kind of love/hate relationship with their new country. They may be grateful to the new country for their freedom and the prosperity they can potentially have there, but they are often unable to accept the new country fully because it cannot provide all the things the refugees lost when they were forced to leave their homeland (Hawthorne, 1982).

Poverty and Economic Concerns

Historically, South Vietnam comprised a largely rural population. Continued communist attempts after World War II to control the rural villages led to a widespread exodus from the land to the cities by South Vietnamese seeking sustenance. By 1974 the homeless rate was 57%, inflation was high, the economy had all but collapsed, and one in seven South Vietnamese was unemployed (Hawthorne, 1982).

Hanoi created New Economic Zones in the South and gave the army responsibility for boosting the economy in rural areas. People were encouraged to return to the land and the New Economic Zones. However, few people were tempted to leave the cities. As difficult as life was in the cities, it was not as harsh as life on the land in the New Economic Zones. The South Vietnamese resisted the government's collective approach to a traditionally family-based working of the land. The economy worsened, and there followed several years of crop failures. Food had to be imported, creating more difficulties, and starvation for many was the result.

Refugees fleeing these conditions found scant relief. In 1977, the median annual income for a Vietnamese in the United States was $9,600, compared with a median annual income for the United States as a whole of $13,572 (Montero, 1979). By 1990 the average annual household income was $15,300, with 4.8 persons per household. The annual per capita income was $3,200, and 35% of families had income below the poverty level (U.S. General Accounting Office, 1990).

When refugees arrived in the United States, unemployment was at a high 9%. Jobs available to Vietnamese were low paying when they existed at all. It was almost impossible for the Vietnamese to save their wages to improve their condition in the United States because of their obligations to send money to Vietnam to help support their extended family who remained there. Economic self-sufficiency was virtually impossible. Available jobs were not only poor paying, they were also low-level positions offering little or no opportunity for advancement. This situation caused emotional crises for Vietnamese and promoted feelings of loss and deprivation, as well as a loss of prestige (Liu & Muralta, 1977). Some 50% of the Vietnamese in the United States in the late 1970s had a secondary education or a university degree; 35% were either without formal education or had only a primary degree (Hawthorne, 1982). By 1990, 62.2% of Vietnamese in the United States over 25 years old had a high school education, and 12.9% had four years of college (U.S. General Accounting Office, 1990).

Economically, Vietnamese refugees have made a quick adjustment in the United States. Their employment picture has steadily improved; in fact, the labor force participation rates of Vietnamese who have been in the United States for five years or longer tend to be higher than those of the general population (Haines, 1985).

History of Oppression

The Vietnamese people have been politically oppressed throughout their history. Until 1940, Vietnam was a part of the French colonial empire. During the Second World War, the French established a government in Vietnam. Ho Chi Minh became the resistance leader.

After the war, Ho Chi Minh declared independence for Vietnam, and France sought restitution of colonial Vietnam. The United States opposed recolonization at first, but later supported France; this move led to the defeat of Vietnam's bid for independence by the mid-1950s.

The Geneva Agreement was to be the signal for peace in Vietnam and the beginning of independence. For the first time, Vietnamese experiencing persecution in the North fled from Ho Chi Minh's regime to the South. At about this time, the United States decided that the pursuit of independence was not correct. No free elections were held, and Diem was put in charge of South Vietnam under U.S. supervision. By 1960 the National Liberation Front had been established in the South to strike at Diem's government as an expression of dissatisfaction with government taxes and attempts to take charge in the villages through the development of Strategic Hamlets.

Diem's assassination signaled the beginning of further U.S. involvement. There were repeated attempts to seize government power and control of the farming communities. A mass exodus by the people to the cities searching for some security and safety followed these attempted coups. The coups ended and a relatively stable political period was the result. Interestingly, this period during the late 1960s was, in fact, a relatively peaceful time for South Vietnam, especially in the rural areas, where the people continued their primitive farming, relatively removed from the upheaval in the cities. This stable time was short, as the National Liberation Front continued to battle in the cities and towns while the United States began withdrawal of troops and aid. American withdrawal afforded the North an opportunity to strengthen its position in the South, and in 1975 the North began to gain control of the South.

The South Vietnamese people were trapped. The protecting U.S. military had deserted them, their rural economy had collapsed, and their leaders were jailed or sent to camps. The refugees began to pour out of South Vietnam into Malaysia, Cambodia, Thailand, Australia, and the United States, seeking relief from the oppression of the communist regime. The largest groups in this movement were the approximately 135,000 people who left abruptly with the U.S. military withdrawal and the 85,000 boat people who left in 1978. Haines (1985) reports that even if the boat people "survived the angry waves, mechanical failure, the lack of food and water, multiple robberies, assaults, and rapes, they still had to suffer humiliation, mistreatment, and possibly internment by the countries of first asylum" (p. 201).

Oppression did not end for these people with flight from their country. Arrival in the United States meant continued economic and personal hardship coupled with a lack of preparation for the cultural differences they encountered. Refugee camps were set up to process these people and resettle them. The Vietnamese were required to remain in the camps until they could meet one of four conditions: (a) They found a sponsor in the United States, (b) they made a decision to return to Vietnam, (c) they could prove they were able to support themselves financially, or (d) they arranged to move to another country, which required verification of that country's willingness to accept them (Hawthorne, 1982).

These were difficult requirements to meet for a number of reasons. The people of the United States did not view the influx of Vietnamese as a favorable event. They blamed these people for the loss of loved ones and the disruption of their lives as a result of the war. The advent of desperate people willing to work at menial tasks for low wages was interpreted by many as a threat to jobs that should go to unemployed U.S. citizens.

Rodriguez and Urrutia-Rojas (1990) describe the host-city rejection suffered by Vietnamese newcomers in the Texas communities of Sea Drift and Seabrook. After settling in Texas between 1976 and 1978, several Vietnamese families left their wage jobs and purchased boats to enter the shrimping business.

Located 18 miles southeast of Houston, the coastal town of Seabrook become a setting of hostilities against Vietnamese refugees. Two Vietnamese fishing boats were burned in the town in February 1981. In the same month, the Ku Klux Klan held an anti-Vietnamese rally in the nearby community of Santa Fe. Armed with rifles, Klan members burned a replica of a Vietnamese fishing boat and vowed to return control of Texas coastal fishing to whites. (p. 274)

A small percentage of the refugees held in camps did, in fact, return to Vietnam. The third and fourth conditions for release from the camps listed above, however, were virtually impossible to meet. Expecting people who had fled their country abruptly and with none of their worldly possessions to show evidence of financial self-sufficiency was ludicrous. And finding a home in another country was equally difficult; these refugees were unwelcome almost everywhere in the world.

Language and the Arts

The Vietnamese language is derived from Chinese. Structurally, the language follows a subject-verb-object pattern similar to English, but the modifier follows the modified term, which is contrary to English structure. The Vietnamese language is noninflectional. There are no form changes in words to denote gender, case, tense, person, or mood. Words in the Vietnamese language tend to be monosyllabic. However, each word has many tones to express differing meanings, such as gravity, evenness, interrogation, or sharpness (Do, 1968). Vietnamese people communicate in a quiet, dignified manner, even when greeting one another. Smiles may cover anger or rejection as well as convey positive warmth and happiness (Dung, 1984).

Vietnamese names are written in the opposite order from English ones. The family name is listed first to emphasize the person's heritage. The middle name is next, and the given name is last. There are no "juniors" in the Vietnamese language. Given names are not shared or passed down from one generation to another. Legally, a woman retains her own name after marriage. Formally, however, she uses only her husband's name preceded by "Mrs."; her own name would not be used (Montero, 1982).

Vietnamese refugees found the language barrier to be a large problem for them in their efforts to acculturate into life in the United States. However, according to Montero (1979), there appears to be no relationship between a proficiency in English and employment figures of Vietnamese Americans.

Vietnamese art dates back to prehistoric times (Whitfield, 1976). Stone and metal works are scarce, because most such works have not survived the climate, wars, and political strife that are part of Vietnamese history. Traditional Vietnamese painting was limited in scope to religious and mythological subjects, evidenced by the abundance of paintings of the four mythological animals: the dragon, the unicorn, the tortoise, and the phoenix.

Vietnamese architecture is reflective of the theme of harmony and unity with nature. The Vietnamese people believe that architecture "should not constitute a struggle against nature, but must instead be in communion with her" (Do, 1968, p. 119). The architecture is often referred to as landscape painting. Sculpture was never a strong Vietnamese art form. The once-popular art of calligraphy, considered a scholarly art form, is no longer widely practiced. The arts of wood carving, ceramics, embroidery, and lacquerware have been highly developed by the Vietnamese.

In general, Vietnamese art reflects the philosophical belief that life on earth is brief. It displays humility, simplicity, and moderation, because grandeur is believed to arise from the spirit, not from physical works of art.

Racism and Prejudice

Race divisions and prejudice are not aspects of life the Vietnamese initially encountered as refugees in America. Historically, the Chinese in Vietnam have been seen as a higher class than the Vietnamese, and they have been attempting to absorb the Vietnamese population for centuries. Do (1968) posits that the Vietnamese race is actually a blending of many racial groups, with a great resemblance among them to Chinese, Koreans, and Japanese. The Vietnamese constitute approximately 80% of the population of Vietnam. Cultural identity is maintained by physical separation in living areas.

The traditional caste system in Vietnam ranks the scholar at the highest level of society. The scholar is followed by the farmer and/or fisherman. The laborer is next, with the merchant or businessman occupying the least esteemed position in the system (Montero, 1982).

After arrival in the United States, the first-wave Vietnamese encountered different forms of racial bias and prejudice than they would have been subjected to in their home country. These refugees were mainly young, financially secure, and among the educationally elite in Vietnam. They were met with resentment for their willingness to accept low-paying, low-level employment while the United States was struggling with economic inflation and high unemployment. The superior education of Vietnamese immigrants was of little use to them in securing employment, housing, and sustenance for their families. Those in the first wave of refugees were also greeted with hostility from U.S. citizens who only wanted to be finished with the Vietnam War and who thus did not welcome any reminders of or association with the Vietnamese people (Montero, 1979).

Sociopolitical Factors

The arrival of Vietnamese in the United States was greeted with resistance of all things Vietnamese because of the war. On the other hand, the Vietnamese, to whom money is not of primary importance, viewed the life-style in the United States as wasteful and luxurious (Hawthorne, 1982). Psychological depression plagued many because of the social and economic pressures of life in the United States. Many Vietnamese lost face, were forced to split from their extended families, and found a culture so different from their own that it was almost impossible for them to reconcile the two.

There had been considerable Western influence in Vietnam for years before the refugees left their country, but, surprisingly, this influence was of little help to the Vietnamese. Even the highly educated were unable to find jobs commensurate with their training; foreign degrees not accepted by American employers, language problems, and the high unemployment level in the United States were all contributing factors. The refugees were concerned about family members left in Vietnam, and needed to share with them financially. Awareness of "Western culture" did not mean automatic acceptance of it, nor did it produce a desire on the part of the Vietnamese to let go of their own cultural heritage.

According to McBee (1984), Vietnamese, Chinese, Japanese, Koreans, and other Asian and Southeast Asian Americans are uniting as a political force to overcome social and economic barriers in this country. They are gaining strength in numbers so that they are able to tilt elections in their favor. For instance, elections in northern Virginia and New Jersey were swayed by their support in 1983 and 1984, respectively. The greatest gains of Asian Americans as officeholders have been in California. Moreover, they are increasingly seeking election in a number of areas across the country. To advance themselves economically, Asian Americans have united to be included in minority "set-aside" allocations of government contracts.

Child-Rearing Practices

In Vietnam, children are considered to be a year old at birth. In rural environments, babies are generally delivered at home, by midwives. Only married women or married female relatives are allowed to attend or assist at births (Montero, 1982).

Sons are more valued than daughters. This belief can be seen as a perpetuation of the centuries-old story of the origin of the Vietnamese people. According to legend, the Vietnamese people are the offspring of the Dragon King and the Fairy Queen, who produced 100 male children. Half of these offspring remained with their mother and went to the mountains to establish a matriarchy. The other half went with their father to the seashore, where a patriarchy was established (Do, 1968). It is interesting to note that the Dragon King and Fairy Queen produced only sons with which to begin the Vietnamese race.

By Western standards, Vietnamese children carry heavy family obligations. The eldest son is responsible for performing ancestor worship at home. Siblings do not kiss or even touch one another, and are usually segregated by sex. Girls are under very strict supervision by family members. Educational achievement is stressed, and there is fierce competition among the children for scholarly progress and success (N. B. Nguyen, 1982).

The Vietnamese child is trained to think of the family first and to subjugate personal desires and concerns. Parents control their children's behavior by appealing to the children's sense of obligation to others. If this sense of obligation is betrayed, a child may be locked outside the house, isolated from social life, shamed, scolded, or made to feel guilty (Morrow, 1987). According to Chan (1986), the use of pride and shame in Vietnamese families is related to the fact that all individual behavior is considered to reflect either positively or negatively on the entire family. Academic and occupational achievement promote family pride, while disobedience, disrespect, and shirking responsibilities promote family shame.

Although the school curriculum in South Vietnam is somewhat similar to a Western configuration, there are still many sharp contrasts between the two. The French, who ruled the country from 1883 to 1954, installed their system of education. Vietnamese children demonstrate respect for teachers by not questioning the teacher's knowledge or authority. They learn by rote memorization, work as a group on one level, and expect large amounts of homework to reinforce learning.

Difficulties can readily be seen for Vietnamese children in schools in the United States. They face multiple problems of adjustment. The language barrier presents a major problem, but cultural differences appear to present the most difficult obstacles. In addition, it is difficult for Vietnamese parents to lend much support to their children in their academic endeavors because of lack of cultural understanding of Western ways and unfamiliarity with the English language.

Religious Practices

Approximately 90% of the Vietnamese people practice some form of Buddhism or ancestor worship (Cohler, 1985). The religious structure is not a separate entity, but a spirituality that pervades all aspects of society. The Vietnamese believe in karma and rebirth; that is, they believe that an individual's life cycle is predetermined by good or bad deeds from a previous life. The goal is eventually to achieve spiritual liberation, or release from the perpetual life and rebirth cycle, by successively living more and more worthy lives. Ancestors are worshiped for four generations after death. Commemoration of a death ceases with the fifth great-grandparents because of the belief that by that time the deceased either have been reborn on earth or have achieved heavenly bliss.

Buddhism, Confucianism, and Taoism have all influenced Vietnamese culture. All have contributed to the ideal of harmony among persons and with nature. Buddhists stress self-discipline and humility, a following of the "middle path." Respect for elders and a hierarchical rank, loyalty, family orientation, loss of face, shame, and regard for education have come from Confucianism. The avoidance of confrontation, an indirect approach to problem solving, patience, and simplicity are taught by Taoism. As a rule, the three religions are not mutually exclusive, and many beliefs are shared among them (Dung, 1984).

Religion for a Vietnamese is not a specific, closed tradition. It is an acceptance of many religions based on the fact that all religions are complementary perspectives on human experience. Persons are to live in harmony with nature without striving to dominate it. What can be considered religious rituals or practices in the United States are part of daily life for the Vietnamese. The central room in a Vietnamese house is often a composite of religious area and living and sleeping quarters. Other evidence of this mixing of family life and religion is seen in the preferred custom of having a marriage take place in the home rather than in a temple or pagoda (Do, 1968).

Very few of the first-wave refugees who came to the United States were Buddhists. Although the Vietnamese Catholic population constituted only 10% of the total number of Vietnamese people, Catholics made up 40% of the refugees in 1975 (Montero, 1979). Do (1968) suggests that the small number of Buddhists willing to relocate in times of political strife may be reflective of the pessimistic and often fatalistic doctrine underlying the Buddhist philosophy.

Since Catholicism is also a part of the Vietnamese culture, immigrants to the United have been able to continue the practice of this religion. As a matter of fact, the Vietnamese-American population has boosted the number of ordained priests in Louisiana (McBee, 1984).

Family Structure and Dynamics

Traditionally, the family has been the basis of Vietnamese society. The family is the core social unit. The extended family is vitally important to the Vietnamese, as are ancestors. Elders are not only supported by children until their deaths, they are also honored and respected for their age and wisdom.

The extended family resides as a single unit, with three or four generations under one roof (Lee & Rong, 1988).

Children remain with the family unit until their marriage. Women marry between the ages of 15 and 25; men marry between 25 and 30 years of age. After her marriage the woman becomes a part of her husband's family and transfers her allegiance and obedience to her spouse and his family. If she is widowed, her eldest son is viewed as the head of the family and is to be obeyed. Until her marriage a woman is submissive to her father.

Traditionally, parents of both the husband-to-be and wife-to-be give approval to the marriage. Divorce is legal but not a common practice among Vietnamese. Most marital difficulties are handled internally by both sides of the family. Until 1959, polygamy was practiced by Vietnamese men. The first wife had primary responsibility for the family, then the second wife, and so forth. All family matters within the household are handled by the wife. The husband attends to all matters related to the outside world.

An extended family of several generations is the norm. The father is the head of the household who supports the family, and the mother manages the household and supervises the education of the children. The Vietnamese usually have many children, so there will be many to provide for them when they get old. Specific roles are designated for family members, and interaction is structured. Females must be submissive; even widows must show deference to their eldest sons. The mother, as the child's first teacher, trains her children in right and wrong conduct. Children are expected to recognize their mistakes, acknowledge them, and take whatever consequences befall, as Buddha taught (Dung, 1984).

With immigration to the United States, the Vietnamese family has undergone tremendous changes. The woman's role has had a dramatic change, as the family seeks to cope with social and economic conditions. The extended family unit has often been split, adding to the adjustment problems facing the Vietnamese American. Large families are still desirable, even in the United States, and one-third of Vietnamese households contain 6 or more people. Some 10% of the Vietnamese families in the United States are made up of 10 or more people. With immigration to the United States, only one marriage was accepted by authorities. This brought about the dissolution of subsequent marriages, but often the additional wives were informally accepted as household members within the family of the first marriage. All members of the Vietnamese family are mutually and reciprocally obligated to the family unit.

Cultural Values and Attitudes

Vietnamese cultural values and attitudes center on the family unit. There is strong emphasis on group loyalty, filial piety, and obedience to elders (S. Nguyen, 1982).

The Vietnamese place a value on controlling their emotions in all situations. Impulsive behavior is to be avoided in an effort to promote harmony. Nonconfrontation is valued as a method of promoting consideration of others. The importance of the individual is insignificant. This attitude can be seen in the Vietnamese positive reinforcement of sacrificial behavior and denial of self-gratification.

Vietnamese are casual in their social arrangements. They approach time in an unhurried, flexible manner. In contrast to this view of the Vietnamese as unhurried and casual, however, Vietnamese refugees expect structure and predictability in social situations (S. Nguyen, 1982). Another indication of a need for structure is the fact that many refugees consider repetition and practice essential for educational progress.

The Vietnamese culture does not emphasize the autonomy of the individual. The family orientation of the Vietnamese promotes individuals with structured mental processes. As mentioned above, Vietnamese also strive for a lack of outward emotional display of feelings. In an open, impulsive culture such as that of the United States, this often makes the Vietnamese seem rather withdrawn and stoic by comparison. Moral virtue and showing respect for more knowledgeable or elderly people is essential for the Vietnamese. Upholding family pride and honor is extremely important, overriding the importance of the individual.

To demonstrate respect or high regard, a Vietnamese person will bow his or her head. When passing an object to a respected person, both hands are used to hold the object. Greetings are given by a Vietnamese by clasping the hands in front of the chest. Vietnamese women never shake hands, even with one another; it has become acceptable in the United States for men to shake hands in greeting. Making direct eye contact while conversing is considered disrespectful (Montero, 1982).

The elderly are the only Vietnamese who can touch another's head publicly, and this is acceptable only if the older person is touching a child's head. However, two Vietnamese of the same sex may hold hands in public or share a bed without any implication of homosexuality. Public kissing is not allowed (Montero, 1982; West, 1984).

Vietnamese do not call to someone considered an equal with a beckoning, finger-up gesture without creating a provocation. The accepted gesture is to use the entire hand with fingers pointed down. Only animals or inferior people are signaled with a finger-up motion.

Implications

Many Vietnamese had no time to prepare psychologically for immigration to the United States. Others suffered trauma as a result of the war, the escape process, and negative conditions in refugee camps. As a result, many psychological disorders have been found among the refugees (Hawthorne, 1982). These disorders are extremely difficult to treat because of the obligation of the Vietnamese to handle problems within the family framework. To seek outside help is to bring embarrassment and shame to the family (Sue, 1981).

Helping professionals who are working with Vietnamese should take the time to become familiar with the basic structural components of the Vietnamese language to facilitate communication and problem solving with clients. Merely learning the order in which a Vietnamese name is written and the implication this form has concerning strong family ties can serve as a reminder to the counselor of the importance of the family to the Vietnamese. It can also demonstrate a sincere desire on the part of the counselor to help by subtly showing respect for this manifestation of a cultural difference.

Tung (1985) recommends that counseling with Vietnamese be of short duration, limited in scope to the problem, goal directed, actively supportive, and focused on the present and immediate future. Lee (1988) recommends a chronological approach to counseling that takes into account the client's life in the homeland, the escape process, and life after arrival in the United States.

Vietnamese disdain for the exuberant life-style of members of the dominant culture of the United States must be viewed in an appropriate manner before effective helping can occur. Displays of respect, restraint of public display of feelings and emotions, lack of eye contact, and reluctance to verbalize a problem should not be construed as signs of distrust or reluctance on the part of the Vietnamese. It is possible that such a client views the counselor as a teacher, in which case he or she will be waiting for the knowledgeable teacher to convey directions and wisdom.

Because of the very nature of the Vietnamese and their reluctance to seek help for problems outside the family unit, the opportunity to counsel them will perhaps be most readily available (or only available) within the school setting, where the Vietnamese may be referred for counseling. The educational system in the United States can cause many difficulties for Vietnamese students as well as for their parents. Appropriate counseling at this level can certainly help. A respect for the value of education is instilled in the Vietnamese virtually from birth, regardless of whether the student comes from the well-educated class or from the poor. Educators must be mindful of this emphasis on educational excellence in dealing with students. The motivation of Vietnamese for academic excellence stems from their strong obligation to the family to do well and bring honor to the home, and the counselor should be aware that their perception of "doing well" often involves a much higher standard than is typical for the average student in the United States.

Language barriers create many problems for the Vietnamese. In a school setting, the language difficulties serve to accentuate the strangeness the student may already feel because of the differences in learning style, classroom structure and management, and curriculum format. An educator must be diligent in explaining these differences and constantly aware that styles of schooling in the United States often seem disrespectful to the Vietnamese. The parents must also be considered when one is counseling students who are experiencing difficulties. Vietnamese parents' concern with their children's success in school is often difficult for them to communicate, and can cause them a great deal of stress and frustration. An effort to orient parents as well as students to the educational structure and system of the dominant culture of the United States seems necessary for effective education. Understanding the composition and importance of the Vietnamese family is, perhaps, the most important component in the education of Vietnamese. As the Vietnamese become more involved in life in the United States and more familiar with the dominant culture, there may be a rejection of their own cultural heritage or a lack of pride and self-confidence. Educators and counselors must be sensitive to areas such as intergenerational and cultural conflicts that arise between Vietnamese parents and children.

An educator or counselor must be aware of and sensitive to the importance of the family to each individual member if teaching and counseling are to be helpful. Exhibiting an appreciation for the differences between the dominant culture and Vietnamese culture can go far toward developing trust and respect.

Questions for Review and Reflection

(1) How might the circumstances surrounding the Vietnam War and the immigration of Vietnamese to the United States influence their degree of acculturation?

(2) What were the major cultural difficulties experienced by the refugees who fled South Vietnam for the United States after 1976? Were these difficulties caused by Vietnamese resistance to acculturation or by resettlement policies of Vietnamese sponsors in the United States?

(3) Why was the immigration of Vietnamese unpopular among many citizens of the United States? What effect did this have on the Vietnamese?

(4) What differences exist between the act of smiling among Vietnamese and among members of the dominant culture? What are the implications of these differences for education or counseling?

(5) What cultural beliefs are reflected in Vietnamese art? How might these values influence the work of educators or counselors working with Vietnamese?

(6) How might the Vietnamese practice of determining age (a child is considered a year old at birth) affect age requirements and restrictions in the dominant culture?

(7) How do children's obligations to the family differ for Vietnamese in the United States and members of the dominant culture in the United States?

(8) What are the implications of the way teachers are treated in Vietnam for the way Vietnamese in the United States may interact with educators or counselors?

(9) Why are Vietnamese often unable to help their children with academic endeavors? How can educators or counselors facilitate Vietnamese parental involvement with academic endeavors?

(10) What is the influence of karma in explaining behaviors of Vietnamese?

References

Chan, S. (1986). Parents of exceptional Asian children. In M. K. Kitano & P. C. Chinn (Eds.), *Exceptional Asian youth* (pp. 36-53). Washington, DC: ERIC.

Cohler, L. (1985, March). New Americans keep old faiths alive. *Scholastic Update,* pp. 17-18.

Cravens, R. B., & Bornemann, T. H. (1990). Refugee camps in countries of first asylum and the North American resettlement process. In W. H. Holtzman & T. H. Bornemann (Eds.), *Mental health of immigrants and refugees* (pp. 38-50). Austin: University of Texas Press.

Do, V. M. (1968). *Viet Nam.* New York: Paragon.

Dung, T. N. (1984). Understanding Asian families: A Vietnamese perspective. *Children Today, 13,* 10-12.

Haines, D. W. (1985). *Refugees in the United States.* Westport, CT: Greenwood.

Hawthorne, L. (1982). *Refugee: The Vietnamese experience.* Melbourne: Oxford University Press.

Lee, E. (1988). Cultural factors in working with Southeast Asian refugee adolescents. *Journal of Adolescence, 11,* 167-179.

Lee, E. S., & Rong, X. (1988). The educational and economic achievement of Asian-Americans. *Elementary School Journal, 9,* 545-560.

Liu, W. T., & Muralta, A. K. (1977). The Vietnamese in America: Perilous flights, uncertain future. *Bridge: An Asian American Perspective, 5,* 42-50.

McBee, S. (1984, April). Asian-Americans: Are they making the grade? *U.S. News & World Report,* pp. 41-47.

Montero, D. (1979). *Vietnamese Americans: Patterns of resettlement and socioeconomic adaptation in the U.S.* Boulder, CO: Westview.

Montero, D. (1982, February). *A mutual challenge.* Paper presented to the U.S. Department of Health, Education and Welfare Region III Task Force.

Morrow, R. D. (1987). Cultural differences: Be aware. *Academic Therapy, 23,* 143-149.

Nguyen, N. B. (1982). *School adjustment of Indochinese students.* Washington, DC: Georgetown University.

Nguyen, S. (1982). The psychosocial adjustment and the mental health of Southeast Asia refugees. *Psychiatric Journal of the University of Ottawa, 7,* 26-38.

Nguyen-Hong-Nhiem, L., & Halpern, J. M. (1989). *The Far East comes near.* Amherst: University of Massachusetts Press.

Office of Refugee Resettlement. (1985). *Refugee resettlement program: Report to the Congress.* Washington, DC: Government Printing Office.

Rodriguez, N. P., & Urrutia-Rojas, X. (1990). Impact of recent refugee migration to Texas: A comparison of Southeast Asian and Central American newcomers. In W. H. Holtzman & T. H. Bornemann (Eds.), *Mental health of immigrants and refugees* (pp. 263-278). Austin: University of Texas Press.

Sue, D. W. (1981). *Counseling the culturally different: Theory and practice.* New York: John Wiley.

Tung, T. M. (1985). *Psychiatric care for Southeast Asians: How different is different?* Washington, DC: U.S. Department of Health and Human Services.

U.S. General Accounting Office. (1990). *Asian Americans: A status report* (Publication No. HRD-90-36FS). Washington, DC: Government Printing Office.

West, B. E. (1984). New students from Southeast Asia. *Education Digest, 49,* 32-35.

Whitfield, D. J. (1976). *Historical and cultural dictionary of Vietnam.* Metuchen, NJ: Scarecrow.

8

Korean Americans

The Korean Americans who live in the United States are among the most recent immigrants to this country. Most of them arrived after 1970 and are middle-class owners of businesses. These people are quite different from the first Koreans who arrived in Hawaii in 1903 to work the sugar and pineapple plantations.

The number of Korean Americans is rapidly increasing. In 1970 there were approximately 70,000 living in the United States. By 1980 that number had increased to 354,529, primarily as a result of revised immigration laws (Hurh & Kim, 1984). Korean Americans represent one of the largest Asian-American groups in the United States today (Ramsey, 1987). It is estimated that by the year 2000, nearly a million Koreans will reside in the United States. Korean Americans are geographically more dispersed than other Asian immigrants, but the heaviest concentration is in Los Angeles. Little is known about Korean Americans because of their small number, which contributes to "general ignorance about [them] as a distinct ethnic group differing significantly from the Chinese and Japanese" (Hurh & Kim, 1984, p. 22).

Acculturation

Patterson (1979), who examined the acculturation process of Korean Americans in Hawaii, feels his analysis is applicable to Koreans in the

United States because of the large concentration of Korean Americans in Hawaii. In his study, he equated upward social mobility with acculturation. The following points made by Patterson illustrate the rapid adjustment and upward mobility of the Koreans:

(1) The diet, dress, and habits of Korean immigrants changed quickly from Oriental to American.

(2) Koreans left plantation work faster than any other ethnic group in the history of Hawaii.

(3) Koreans recorded one of the highest rates of urbanization.

(4) Koreans generally spoke better English than the Japanese or Chinese.

(5) Second-generation Korean children were staying in school longer than any other ethnic group, including Chinese, Japanese, and Caucasian.

(6) Second-generation Koreans recorded one of the highest rates of professionalism.

(7) Second-generation Koreans exhibited more liberal and egalitarian attitudes toward social issues than Chinese-Americans or Japanese-Americans.

(8) By the early 1970s, the Koreans had achieved the highest per capita income and the lowest unemployment rate of any ethnic group in Hawaii, including Caucasians. (p. 83)

Because of their small numbers, Koreans in Hawaii were forced to mingle with other ethnic groups. This is one part of the explanation for their rapid acculturation. Other data reveal that Korean immigrants differed markedly from their countrymen in five areas. The first of these was religion. In a country where traditional orthodoxy was based upon Buddhism and Confucianism, the majority of Korean immigrants to Hawaii were connected in some way to Christianity. The second area of difference was demographics. Most immigrants came from urbanized areas, yet the majority of Korea is rural. The third area is occupation. Most Koreans were peasant farmers, yet the majority of immigrants were government clerks, political refugees, students, policemen, miners, woodcutters, household servants, and Buddhist monks. The fourth departure from the norm was the fact that the immigrants may have been better educated than their countrymen. The fifth important difference between the immigrants and other Koreans was their nontraditional value system. Armed conflicts, drought, famine, and oppressive taxes forced people to abandon the countryside for the uncertainties of the city. In the cities young refugees came to embrace cosmopolitan, modern, and antitraditional liberal influences. Forced to abandon the graves of their ancestors and therefore the required Confucian rituals, they became primary candidates for conversion to Christianity and other influences of the culture in the United States (Patterson, 1979).

Hurh (1980) describes Korean-American acculturation in a model that emphasizes that *Korean* and *American* are not mutually exclusive categories. Hurh describes Korean Americans as "pluralist," both Korean and American; "integrationist," holding Korean values but trying to be more American; "traditionalist," more Korean than American; or "isolationist," neither Korean nor American.

One group that faces unique challenges of adjustment to the culture of the United States is made up of those who are "1.5 generation Korean Americans" (Lee & Cynn, 1991). These Korean Americans were born in Korea but have spent most of their life in the United States. Their adjustment difficulties center on differences in the rate of their acculturation and that of their immigrant parents. The 1.5-generation Korean Americans are young, mobile, and quick in adapting to values of the dominant culture in the United States. These characteristics place them in conflict with their parents and the traditional values of the Korean culture.

While Koreans have acculturated to some extent, there are barriers that they must overcome to do so. The family-centered, traditional Korean immigrant finds the free-style, aggressive, individualistic way of life in the United States incompatible with that of the homeland. The language barrier is a hurdle even for those who learned some English before leaving Korea. Most do not have time to take English classes because they are working hard to survive. Thus some have a tendency to isolate themselves from the dominant culture and stay within the Korean community.

Poverty and Economic Concerns

The first wave of Korean immigrants came to Hawaii to work on the sugar cane plantations. Economic improvement for the early Korean immigrants was difficult, because they were exploited by plantation owners, whose main concern was profit. Although they were not contract laborers, the language barrier, racial discrimination, and cultural conflicts prevented them from obtaining more gainful employment consistent with their individual abilities and skills. The first generation worked hard and saved, to ensure that their children would receive a good education. Many eventually opened their own businesses. By the 1970s, Koreans in Hawaii had higher per capita income than all other groups, including Caucasians (Patterson, 1979).

Koreans helped one another financially. Communities or groups of tradesmen would organize *qyes* (revolving credit unions) to look after their own. This helped to improve the economic status of the group as a whole.

While many Korean Americans today are underemployed as a result of language barriers and racial discrimination, few receive public assistance.

The newer immigrants seem to be respecting the pattern of the first immigrants, establishing independent businesses.

Unlike earlier immigration patterns, there is now a different kind of Korean coming to the United States. The most recent immigrants are primarily extremely wealthy Koreans from South Korea. They, of course, are not faced with economic hardship in the United States.

History of Oppression

Korea is a land with a long history of oppression. The Korean peninsula is surrounded by three powerful countries—China, Russia, and Japan. Koreans have been subject to oppression both in their native country and in the United States, where they came to escape oppression. A capsulized version of Korea's history will illustrate this.

The traditional view about the origin of the Korean people is based on legend. Tradition places the founding of the tribal state in the year 2333 B.C., with the descent of Tan'gun-wanggom, a spirit king of divine origin. His successors reigned for 1,200 years. Although there is no archaeological evidence to support this story, some Korean historians write about it nonetheless.

According to anthropologists, the Korean people are descended partly from the Mongolian race and partly from the Tungus and Proto-Caucasoids who arrived from the plains of Manchuria or central Asia. Koreans suffered from almost unbearable exploitation and humiliation under the Mongols, and national strength and resources were gradually exhausted.

During the seventeenth and eighteenth centuries there was considerable factionalism within the ruling class based on southern versus northern provincialism, and fights over the division of land developed. The traditional Confucianists and the neo-Confucianists were also at odds. The ultimate struggle was for monopoly of political power by one group. This factionalism weakened the government and hindered social and economic progress. The ruling class had developed a reliance upon China as a safeguard for independence. They hoped that China would provide a buffer from the outside world since China treated Korea as a tributary state. The Yi Dynasty did not develop any foreign policy of its own and was ill prepared to defend against the events during the last 25 years of the nineteenth century (Choy, 1979).

The French in 1866 and the United States in 1871 tried to open the doors to the "Hermit Kingdom" without success. Isolation ended, however, when Japan and Korea entered into a treaty of friendship and commercial trade. By 1882 Korea signed a similar treaty with the United States. Soon European nations also entered into diplomatic relations with Korea. With the end of isolation, Korea became a battleground of political strife in the Far East. As its social, economic, and political feudal system disintegrated, revolts took place in 1882, 1884, and 1894. The last revolt led to a Japanese invasion, which in turn resulted in the Sino-Japanese War of 1894-1895.

Following the end of World War II in 1945, the U.S. Army established a military government in South Korea while the Russians occupied the North. The Republic of Korea was formed in the South in 1948. By 1949 the People's Republic of Korea was formed. On June 25, 1950, hostilities broke out on the border at the thirty-eighth parallel, launching the Korean War.

The experience of Koreans in the United States was similar to that of Japanese and Chinese immigrants—they all faced economic hardships and were victimized by the anti-Oriental movements on the West Coast. Their economic ventures were greatly limited by racial discrimination.

The National Origins Act of 1924 closed the door on Korean immigration for almost 40 years. The Immigration Act of 1965 once again allowed entry of Koreans who had close relatives in the United States or who possessed specific skills defined as contributing to the growth of the U.S. economy.

Language and the Arts

The Korean language is of the Ural-Altaic language family, which also includes Japanese, Turkish, Mongolian, and Manchu. Despite the fact that the official writing system of the Korean government for many years was that of the Chinese, the Koreans never adopted the Chinese language, although they did borrow some words from it. There are dialect differences between North and South Korea, but they are not sufficiently large to provide a barrier to understanding. During the reign of King Sejong (1397-1450) a royal commission of scholars, after many years of study, developed a Korean alphabet. This took place during the early years of the Yi Dynasty. The Korean alphabet is phonetic and consists of 19 consonants, 8 vowels, and 2 semivowels. This phonetic system was credited to the personal leadership of the king and was called *hunmin jongum.* Today it is named *Han'gul,* and it is the oldest known alphabet of its kind still in use. Considered an inferior system by the Confucian scholar-officials, Han'gul was little used until revived by missionaries in the nineteenth century. Suppressed by the Japanese during their years of Japanese occupation, Han'gul was adopted in 1945 as the official written language. Both North and South Korea have endorsed Han'gul to symbolize their nationalism. The invention of this alphabet is held in such high regard that a national holiday celebrates the event.

In any language there are spoken and unspoken ways that express the speaker's attitude toward the person about whom or to whom the speech is addressed. Korean has grammatical devices specifically for this purpose.

Use of an inappropriate sociolinguistic level of speech is socially unacceptable and is normally interpreted as having a special message such as intended formality (e.g., use of the honorific level when familiar level is acceptable) or disrespect or contempt to a social superior (e.g., use of the familiar level when the honorific is appropriate). One sometimes may have to evaluate the degree of intimacy with the speech partner before choosing an appropriate level of formality from among the four different levels of speech (higher honorific, simple honorific, simple familiar, and lower familiar). This speech system is an important linguistic feature characterizing interpersonal relationships in the Korean culture.

By elementary school, children have acquired the basic rules of honorifics. If a child does not know how to choose an appropriate level of speech in a given situation, the child's parents are blamed for poor home education, and the child's speech is branded as "baby talk." Many Korean immigrant parents point out that if their children have not acquired the honorifics system, they avoid using Korean whenever possible.

Another distinctive aspect of Korean language is the treatment of names. There are only 232 surnames in all of Korea. More than 53% of the population has one of the five major surnames: Kim, Lee/Rhee/Yi, Park, Choi/Choe, or Chung/Jung.

Each individual name has two Chinese characters, one of which identifies the generation, and the other of which is the individual's personal name. For example, in a family three children may be named Kim Sung Shik, Kim Sung Ja, and Kim Sung Chul. Kim is the surname, Sung is for the generation, and Shik, Ja, and Chul are the individuals' names. Sometimes the generation names are reversed, but the surname always comes first. Because of the rule in English that surnames come last, Korean family names and personal names are often confused by Americans.

The art of Korea is reflected in its music and dance. There are two kinds of music in Korea. Court ceremonial music is solemn and dignified, and is written. The second type is folk music, which is usually fast and lively. One traditional folk song is the farmer's song, which is basically a prayer for a good harvest. There is also a traditional form of performing art, called *pansori*.

A typical Korean musical instrument is the *kayaqeum*, which was invented during the Silla period. It is a 12-string harp-type instrument played with the fingers. Usually played by women, it produces a melancholy sound.

Korean dances are expressions of wishes for good luck, wealth, and rich harvests. There are many kinds of dances, of which the drum dance is typical. It is performed by a woman who beats a drum that is slung across her shoulder. There is also another type of drum dance in which a number of drums, sitting in two rows, are beaten by the dancer in various tempos and rhythms.

Korean folk songs are different from those of other Asian countries. First of all, women are credited with the writing of many folk songs. The songs are an emotional outlet for them and express their feelings about being oppressed by men. Another characteristic of Korean folk songs is the humor that is used to turn a sad occasion into a lighter event. Of all Korean folk songs the best known is the "Arirang," which is the name of a mountain pass. It was very popular with Korean underground patriots when the Japanese dominated Korea. Japanese authorities banned the singing of the Korean national anthem, so freedom-loving Koreans expressed their patriotism by singing the "Arirang."

Racism and Prejudice

Most immigrant groups are discriminated against shortly after their arrival in the United States, yet with some groups prejudice tends to fade away. Overt prejudice appears to diminish as a group assimilates into the dominant culture of the United States. Korean Americans faced racism and prejudice upon their arrival in this country and they continue to face it at the covert level. Most American-born Korean Americans have achieved high levels of education and are able and qualified professionals, but racial discrimination sometimes prevents their finding jobs consistent with their abilities. Virtually no Korean American holds a position as a business executive in a large American corporation (those without Korean ties). Almost no Korean lawyers work in large American law firms. The most conspicuous areas of underemployment are in the field of medicine (doctors, dentists, nurses), in architecture, and in pharmacy. As of 1979, Choy estimated that only 5% of Korean Americans were doing what they were trained for.

Although the United States gives preferential admission to persons of select professional classes, U.S. licensing agencies are discriminatory against foreign professionals. Consequently, the only option available for many Korean Americans is to start their own businesses.

Sociopolitical Factors

Most of the sociopolitical factors in Korean-American culture are the result of the political turmoil in their homeland and efforts of the immigrants to aid in the movement for independence.

The National Origins Act of 1924, an effort to increase the number of European immigrants, prevented Koreans from entering the United States. The Immigration Act of 1965 and its 1976 amendment determined both the number and social characteristics of acceptable Korean immigrants—their sex, age, occupation, and education (Kim, 1981).

The church has become the primary social organization among Korean Americans. Kim (1981) reports that two anti-Park (South Korean President Park Chung-hee) associations, the Korean American Political Association, and the Korean American Chamber of Commerce, were founded in New York City.

Child-Rearing Practices

Acceptable norms for behavior in the Korean family and society are strongly influenced by the teachings of Confucius, a Chinese philosopher. Much of Confucianism focuses on the need to maintain social order through nurturing and preserving the "five relationships": between parents and children, between older persons and younger persons, between husband and wife, between friends, and between ruler and subject (which includes the teacher-student relationship). Interest in preserving these relationships is quite prevalent among Korean Americans and should be noted by those involved with teaching and counseling this group. Each of these relationships is hierarchical and dictates appropriate behavior.

> A son should be reverential; a younger person respectful; a wife submissive; a subject loyal. And, reciprocally, a father should be strict and loving; an older person wise and gentle; a husband good and understanding; a ruler righteous and benevolent; and friends trusting and trustworthy. In other words, one is never alone when one acts since every action affects someone else. (Kim, 1981, p. 11)

There is a strong emphasis on preserving family honor among Koreans. If a child behaves in an embarrassing manner, the whole family is disgraced. A child in a Korean family is hardly regarded as an independent, whole person. Most decisions directly or indirectly affecting children are made by the parents or other older members of the family. Children are not encouraged to express their opinions; insistence on doing so in an exchange with a superior results in a scolding. Vocal expression of personal wishes is seldom rewarded. Children are expected to remain quiet, particularly in the presence of adults.

Typical Korean-American parents are in their late 30s, usually have two or three children of elementary school age, and most often have a high school or college education. In most households, both parents are employed full-time outside the home, in contrast to the life pattern in Korea. The parents' expectations for their children in school, in both academic and social areas, are very high.

Religious Practices

The majority of Korean Americans embrace some form of Christianity. Indeed, religion played an integral part in the history of Korean immigration to the United States. Missionaries from the United States played an important role in persuading Koreans to immigrate to Hawaii.

The first American minister in Seoul, a physician-missionary sent by the Presbyterian Board of Foreign Missions of the United States, became one of the most trusted of the Korean king's advisers. After his successful treatment of the queen's nephew, who was wounded during a political coup in 1884, he became the royal family's personal physician. Thus he was able to persuade the king to permit his subjects to immigrate to Hawaii (Choy, 1979). On the day the first group of immigrants left Korea, he went to the port and offered his prayers for the safety of the immigrants to the strange land. He also handed a few of the leaders among them letters of introduction to the superintendent of the Methodist Mission in Hawaii. Therefore, there were already Christians among the first Korean immigrants to Hawaii, and a few of them were preachers.

The period between 1903 and 1918 saw rapid growth in the number of Koreans professing Christianity. Methodist, Episcopal, and Presbyterian churches were established. A number of factors seem to have contributed to this growth. First, Korean society in Hawaii lacked strong social groups established on the basis of traditional ties. Second, Christianity may have served as a means of communicating to the dominant culture that the Koreans were attempting to assimilate. Third, the church offered those who were not members of other associations their only opportunity to engage in social intercourse outside the work camps. Fourth, there seems to have been a certain degree of pressure on non-Christians to convert, particularly after a significant number of Koreans had become converts. Parents who were not Christians sent their children to church (Choy, 1979).

The period between 1919 and 1925 was marked by disputes over policy on church administration, church financial business, and the operation of the Korean boarding school later known as the Central Institute. In the fall of 1916 a group of 70 or 80 people left their Methodist church to begin what became known as the Korean Christian church. They were seeking independence and self-government. Members of the Korean Christian church were an indispensable part of the Korean national independence movement abroad. They asserted that Korea was ready for independence and self-government. Financial contributions were given for these purposes. The Korean Christian church eventually became so politically oriented that the spirituality of its members was no longer addressed. Church services became political meetings.

The Korean Christian church had its own share of internal dissent. There was a faction who wished for the church to once again become a place of worship. Feelings ran so high that force was used and violence occurred. Almost every Sunday, local police were called in. The controversy was settled by the court, which ordered the two groups to unite in October 1948.

The third period in the history of the church in the Korean-American community (1946 to 1967) was characterized by an effort by the first generation to maintain the status quo, and by an attitude of indifference and rebellion on the parts of the second and third generations. To the first generation the church was a place of both social interaction and cultural identification. Their traditional language, values, and customs were reinforced through social contacts provided by the church. The second and third generations did not share the language or culture of the first generation. It should also be noted that between 1924 and 1968, as mentioned above, the exclusion law and quota system in immigration policy prevented more Koreans from coming to the United States.

The fourth period of history for the church in the Korean-American community began with the influx of new immigrants after 1965. This new wave of immigration promises resources and leadership long needed for a revival of the ethnic church in the Korean-American community. This leadership may not, however, be channeled into existing ethnic churches. Since new immigrants arriving in the United States have their own religious preferences, they often look for churches of their own choice or try to establish their own denominational churches (Choy, 1979).

With the exception of holding services in Korean, the churches of Korean Americans and those within the dominant culture do not seem to differ a great deal.

Family Structure and Dynamics

Koreans have generally immigrated in their basic social unit, the nuclear family. Frequently a family is temporarily separated so that a pioneer member can establish an economic base, or because of a bureaucratic delay under U.S. or Korean immigration laws. Favorable conditions for continuing the old family unit or creating a new family life in the United States were fostered by the Immigration Act of 1965, which permitted reunion of immediate relatives.

The majority of Korean householders are married, with the eldest male, usually the husband, considered head of the household. This family structure contrasts with that prevalent among older Korean immigrants, who encountered an immigration law hostile to the creation of families. Even the solution of "picture brides" was not a permanent answer for the extreme shortage of females among older Korean immigrants. Now the opposite phenomenon, a female surplus in the marriage market, has occurred largely due to the selective immigration policy of the government of the United States.

Since Korean women outnumber Korean men in the United States, marriageable women face a serious problem in finding husbands. They are further handicapped in that Korean men, still concerned with the traditional Korean virtue of female chastity, tend to distrust acculturated Korean women, who, they think, are too aggressive and disobedient. Thus there has been a strong tendency among eligible men to take month-long trips to their home country to "pick out a brand-new bride" (Kim, 1981, p. 45). Immigrant Korean women have resorted to the same technique. Both groups have been successful in their marriage ventures because "homeland Koreans are crazy about the Korean-Americans" (Kim, 1981, p. 45). When negotiating for their South Korean spouses, Korean Americans tend to inflate their status in the United States. These marriage ventures have facilitated "kinship-centered" immigration because, after marrying in South Korea, Korean Americans have filed for "family reunion" visas upon returning to the United States. A higher proportion of Korean immigrants send for their entire families once they have acquired citizenship. Spouses and children can enter under "family reunion" visas, but once citizenship is obtained other close relatives can also be brought to the United States.

Almost all Korean immigrant families belong to a modified extended-family group. This group includes several nuclear families and is based on the husbands' or wives' common schooling or work experiences in the old or new land, rather than on actual kinship. These groups have also emerged from living in the same neighborhoods or from having identical hobbies. These family associations are different from an extended family. They are informal and have few traditions and rituals. At most, they are substitutes for the extended family, designed for the exchange of material and emotional support. During special occasions such as Christmas, New Year's Eve, and Chinese New Year's Day, they usually meet to enjoy Korean food, dancing, and talk. In many cases, family groups or associations also function as a *gye,* a Korean equivalent of a rotating credit association.

Cultural Values and Attitudes

Korean cultural values and attitudes can perhaps best be illustrated by contrasting them with those of the dominant culture:

Dominant culture	*Korean-American culture*
emphasize individual autonomy	emphasize family
internal frame of reference (autonomy)	external frame of reference (obedient to elders)
all people equal	people ranked in a hierarchy

informal personal relationships	formal personal relationships
student-centered learning	teacher-centered learning
(free to question)	(do not question)
students problem solve	students memorize
equality of sexes	male dominance

According to Sue (1981), Asian Americans in general tend to take a more practical approach to life and problems than do Caucasians. Well-structured and predictable situations are preferred over ambiguous ones. Asian Americans also appear less autonomous; more dependent, conforming, and obedient to authority; more inhibited, less ready to express impulses, more law-abiding, less assertive, and more reserved. There is a strong cultural emphasis on suppression of strong feelings, obedience to family authority, and subjugation of individuality to the benefit of the family. Asian Americans are less extroverted than Caucasians. The cultural influence on formality in interpersonal relations may make Asians uncomfortable when interacting with the more spontaneous and informal dominant culture. Asian cultures are family centered and tend to view outsiders with suspicion. Asians have suffered the effects of racism in the United States, and this reinforces mistrust. All of these points concerning Asian Americans in general are applicable to Korean Americans.

Whereas the dominant culture of the United States stresses the importance of the individual first, Korean Americans stress family, community, culture, and global influences. Throughout their years in the United States, many Korean Americans have played an active role in the independence movement in Korea.

Implications

Korean cultural values may inhibit Korean Americans from seeking counseling services even when they are feeling psychological distress. Public admission of personal problems is suppressed, and restraint of strong feelings is encouraged. Seeking counseling may be perceived as bringing shame and disgrace upon one's family. Physical complaints may be an expression of emotional difficulties.

An awareness of family relationships will help teachers and counselors understand the respect that Korean-American parents and students have for teachers and other school officials. This awareness will help counselors become sensitive to many Korean-American expectations for guidance and direction. Since Korean Americans are reared believing that their actions will inevitably affect others, they want to ensure that their impact on others will be as they intend it.

Counselors and educators should be aware that Korean Americans who seek help may experience guilt and shame because of it. Confidentiality is a factor to be dealt with immediately. The presenting problem may not be the real problem, but a manifestation of something deeper. To build trust and rapport, counselors should deal with the superficial problems first, as they are likely to be less threatening to the client. Helping professionals need to employ a logical, structured, directive approach when dealing with Korean Americans.

Questions for Review and Reflection

(1) What factors contributed to Korean Americans' rapid adjustment and upward mobility in the United States? Which of these factors are most consistent with values in the dominant culture of the United States? Which are most inconsistent?

(2) How has the size of the Korean-American population affected the group's acceptance in the United States?

(3) How does the Korean linguistic system influence the communication of Korean Americans in the dominant culture?

(4) What information is contained in the order of names of Korean Americans? How is this different from the English system of naming?

(5) What knowledge of family relationships among Korean Americans is useful to educators and counselors? How does the concept of "family honor" affect the rearing of children in the Korean-American culture?

(6) How has acculturation affected the number of Korean-American women who marry Korean-American men? What effect does this phenomenon have on the maintenance of the Korean-American culture?

(7) Korean-American culture is said to emphasize an "external frame of reference." How does this value affect Korean Americans and their interactions with the dominant culture?

(8) What are the implications for educators and counselors of Korean-American students' teacher-centered learning style?

(9) How can educators and counselors intervene with Korean Americans who are psychologically distressed when the Korean-American culture inhibits them from seeking help outside the family?

(10) What unique problems might one expect Korean Americans to experience in comparison with other Asian-American groups?

References

Choy, B. (1979). *Koreans in America.* Chicago: Nelson-Hall.

Hurh, W. M. (1980). Towards a Korean-American ethnicity: Some theoretical models. *Ethnic and Racial Studies, 3,* 444-464.

Hurh, W. M., & Kim, K. C. (1984). *Korean immigrants in America.* Rutherford, NJ: Fairleigh Dickinson University Press.

Kim, I. (1981). *New urban immigrants: The Korean community in New York.* Princeton, NJ: Princeton University Press.

Lee, J. C., & Cynn, V. E. H. (1991). Issues in counseling 1.5 generation Korean Americans. In C. C. Lee & B. B. Richardson (Eds.), *Multicultural issues in counseling: New approaches to diversity* (pp. 127-140). Alexandria, VA: American Association for Counseling and Development.

Patterson, W. (1979). Upward social mobility of the Koreans in Hawaii. *Korean Studies, 3.*

Ramsey, R. S. (1987). Teaching Korean in America today. In R. A. Morse (Ed.), *Wild asters: Explorations in Korean thought, culture and society.* Lanham, MD: University Press of America.

Sue, D. W. (1981). *Counseling the culturally different: Theory and practice.* New York: John Wiley.

9

Mexican Americans

The Mexican-American culture is a mix of Spanish, Indian, and American cultures. The Mexican American identifies with all three but is set apart from all three cultures by language, race, and religion.

Among the choices for identity for individuals in this culture are Mexican American, Chicano, La Raza, Mestizo, Spanish American, Spanish surnamed, Native American, and Spanish speaking. *Mexican American* implies that anyone who might identify with the population has origins in what is now Mexico, a fact that may or may not be true. *Chicano* was once used as a derisive term and is therefore still offensive to some, but has become a source of pride for social and political activists in recent decades. *La Raza* translates literally as "the race" and includes all peoples of the Americas with some Spanish cultural roots (Meier & Rivera, 1981). It is also widely used as a source of cultural pride. *Mestizo* refers to a person of mixed Indian and European ancestry, either racially or culturally. *Spanish American* denies the Native American ancestry and culture, while *Native American* denies the Spanish ancestry and cultural contributions. Those who choose to use terms such as *Spanish speaking* or *Spanish surnamed* have been considered by activists to be more acculturated into the dominant Anglo culture. Thus, while those in this population share some common experiences and culture, they do not share a common identity.

Matute-Bianchi (1986) identifies five major categories of ethnic identity within the Mexican-American student population: (a) recent Mexican immigrant (Mexican-born, Spanish-speaking, "Mexicano" identity), (b) Mexican oriented (bilingual, strong ties to both Mexico and the United States, disavows identity as "Mexican American"), (c) Mexican American (born in the United States, assimilated, prefers English over Spanish), (d) Chicano (identify as Mexican or Mexicano, alienated from mainstream-oriented activities), and (e) cholo (marginal, disaffected, frequently associated with gangs).

For this chapter, the term *Mexican American* will be used to refer to a citizen of the United States either by birth or naturalization who is of Mexican descent, usually of mixed European (largely Spanish) and Native American (Indian) origins (Meier & Rivera, 1981). This term also includes those Mexicans and Native Americans whose homeland is the American Southwest and Texas and whose culture and language are Spanish influenced.

The criteria for identification as Mexican American have changed from census to census (born in Mexico, parents born in Mexico, Spanish speaking, Spanish surname, and so on). Defining Mexican Americans is a complex task, involving not only their varied history, languages, nativity, and social and economic integration in the United States, but also their own perception of ethnicity (Hurtado & Arce, 1987). The main problem in defining the U.S. population of Mexican descent is its heterogeneity combined with its sociopolitical history.

Mexican Americans account for 60% of the Hispanic population in the United States, which is projected to be the largest minority group by the year 2000 (accounting for 11-12% of the total population) (Church, 1985). Despite having contributed to the gross national product, paid taxes, and actively supported U.S. military activity since 1848, they struggle to be acknowledged as worthy, productive individuals with equal rights.

Arias (1986) calls the rapid growth of the Hispanic population in the United States one of the "most compelling social developments in the last 25 years" (p. 27). No longer a rural group, Hispanics represent a significant number of metropolitan residents. In 1985, Mexican Americans numbered more than 10 million. The majority of Mexican Americans, some 73% of all Mexican Americans in the United States, live in California and Texas.

Historically the Mexican Americans are a conquered people, beginning with Spain's invasion of Mexico in the 1600s and ending with the annexation of Mexican territories by the United States in 1848 (Kiskadden & Rossell, 1979). It is important to understand that they were already living in what today constitutes the southwestern United States before Manifest Destiny took over and made them a minority group with minimal rights. As the Anglo population expanded West, settlers came to live within the Mexican territories, and at that time expressed loyalty to the Mexican culture. For 10 to 15 years, they lived peacefully and in cooperation with their Mexican neighbors. Conflict developed as the Mexicans struggled internally over government rule and the United States became anxious to increase its territory. Many Mexicans fought with the Americans to achieve the independent state of Texas, but soon found themselves foreigners as the Mexican government ceded the southwestern territories to the United States under the Treaty of Guadalupe Hidalgo. Hence they became Mexican by birth, language, and culture and citizens of the United States by the might of arms (Ortego, 1973).

For the Mexican American, immigration from Mexico was motivated by a desire for change and opportunity. A heavy value is placed on the need for challenge and achievement. However, prejudice and discrimination against Mexican Americans shut off many of the usual avenues to achievement. Damaging stereotypes, such as Mexicans being lazy, passive, and failure oriented, have been reinforced by society and the media. These stereotypes have become internalized by some Mexican Americans who have lost contact with their ancestral culture. On the other hand, Mexican Americans who are integrated with their traditional culture have a more positive image of themselves and of their group. Consequently, these persons are in a better position to make headway against prejudice and discrimination and thereby increase their chances for success.

As it is important for Mexican Americans not to disregard their heritage, it is also important for the Anglo culture to regard this culture as valuable. As Anglos expect the Mexican American to learn the dominant culture, it is also important for Anglos to possess an understanding of the Mexican-American culture.

Acculturation

Acculturation is best described as an adjustment process whereby, as a result of sociocultural interactions, a person acquires the customs of an alternate culture. Many Mexican Americans today have a low degree of acculturation as a result of two factors. First, they are descendants of relatively recent immigrants or are immigrants themselves. Second, most other immigrant groups with large numbers of acculturated members arrived in one or more waves and subsequently successfully acculturated. Mexican immigration has been more like a steady stream, inhibiting the acculturation of residents of longer standing.

Alvarez (1973) describes Mexican Americans as

a creation of the imperial conquest of one nation by another through military force. Our people were thrown into a new set of circumstances, and began to evolve new modes of thought and action in order to survive making Mexican-American culture different from the culture of Mexicans in Mexico. Because we live in different circumstances we have evolved different cultural modes; just as we are neither identical to "Anglos" in the United States nor to Mexicans in Mexico, we nevertheless incorporate into our ethos much from both societies. This is because we respond to problems of existence that confront us in unique ways, distinct from the way in which Anglos and Mexicans experience them. (p. 938)

Hernandez and Carlquist-Hernandez (1979) use a three-category system to classify Mexican Americans' degree of acculturation. The "traditional" Mexican American identifies strongly with family, community, ethnic group, and members of the extended family. The "duotraditional" Mexican American is semiurban, ethnically heterogeneous, and has moderate ties to his or her family. The "atraditional" Mexican American has been assimilated into the community at large, has few familial ties, is urban, and speaks English as his or her primary language.

Many Mexican Americans have tended to remain separate and less mobile by choice. Like other ethnic groups, they have often found this the easier course, since they need not strain to learn another language or to change their ways and manners.

Although Mexican Americans may remain separate, they share some of the patterns of living of Anglo-American society. The demands of life in the United States have required basic modifications of Mexican cultural tradition. Materially, Mexican Americans are not much different from Anglos. Mexicans have acquired English in varying degrees, and their Spanish has become noticeably Anglicized. Although the original organization of the family has persisted, major changes have occurred in patterns of traditional authority, as well as in child-rearing and courtship practices. Still, the Mexican American retains the more subtle characteristics of Mexican heritage, particularly in the conception of time and in other fundamental value orientations, as well as the mode of participation in interpersonal relations.

Many of the most acculturated Mexican Americans have become largely Anglo-American in their way of living, but they retain fluent Spanish and a knowledge of their traditional culture. They maintain an identification with their own heritage while participating in Anglo-American culture. Mexican-American culture represents the most constructive and effective means its members have of coping with their changed natural and social environment. They exchange old ways for new ways only if the new ways appear to be more meaningful and rewarding than the old, and then only if they are given full opportunity to acquire and use the new ways.

Poverty and Economic Concerns

Mexican Americans are an economically disadvantaged group. By standards of the dominant culture, they have experienced little social progress, even though they have lived in the southwestern United States longer than most other ethnic groups. As a result of a particular approach to life and distinct cultural values, which are usually viewed as opposite to Anglo-American values, Mexican Americans have been prevented from succeeding in the United States because of discrimination by Anglo society (Duran & Bernard, 1973). Mexican Americans find themselves markedly behind in total amount of education, occupations, income, housing, political representation, and professional identification. At the time of the 1980 census, 19% of Mexican-origin families lived below the poverty line, in comparison with 9% of the Anglo population. Miller, Nicolau, Orr, Valdivieso, and Walker (1988) report that in 1985, Hispanic per capita income had fallen below that of African Americans, with $6,613 for Hispanics, $6,840 for African Americans, and $11,671 for whites and Asian Americans. In 1985 the average number of school years completed by Hispanics 25 years old or older was 11.5, while the general population had completed 12.6 years. In 1980, 74% of all 17-year-olds in the United States had high school diplomas, while only 40% of Hispanics had graduated from high school (Arias, 1986).

Social scientists who study Mexican Americans invariably end up describing poor Mexican Americans. Those qualities that have been invariably attributed to Mexican Americans as part of their ethnicity are actually those of people in poverty, but that regularly cut across ethnic lines.

Mexican Americans have never been unconscious of the conditions of poverty, disease, hunger, and ignorance in which they live, and have never been unconscious of the fact that they were forced to live under such conditions in an exploitative society. The problems are "caused by the Anglo society and are not found within the culture itself" (Duran & Bernard, 1973, p. 2).

History of Oppression

Mexican Americans have been reliving the epitome of the immigrant experience in the United States. They come out of distress; they speak an alien tongue; they suffer the uncertainties of the newcomer; they are exploited by their own countrymen who contract their labor and are then exploited again by the employer to whom they are peddled; they are the underclass on whom others look down; they are disproportionately underpaid, uneducated, unacculturated, and unwanted.

In the years following Mexican independence from Spain in 1821, the northern areas of the new nation (now the U.S. Southwest) were centers of unrest. Santa Anna tried to impose a central focus on the country that made the outer reaches of the north uneasy.

In brief wars and a series of conflicts that fell just short of being "official" wars, Mexican Americans were the "enemy." The first war was the War for

Texas Independence in 1835 and the second was the Mexican War of 1846. The war between Mexico and the United States formally ended with the Treaty of Guadalupe Hidalgo in 1848. But that did not end the actual fighting. Force was used by the Anglos to gain control, and force was used by the Mexicans to retaliate. In New Mexico, an abortive rebellion followed the American occupation.

In the twentieth century, during the Mexican Revolution of 1910-1920, hostility between the two countries culminated in the occupation of Veracruz by U.S. forces in 1914, and the famous "Punitive Expedition" into Chihuahua led by Pershing in search of Pancho Villa after the latter's raid on Columbus, New Mexico. Because Mexico was the foe, Mexican Americans suffered indignities.

The Anglo-Americans who began to enter New Mexico found that commerce and access to the natural resources of the land were the means to power and wealth. Within a few years after the American conquest, Anglo-American and Mexican-American merchants were found in virtually all of the larger Mexican-American villages. However, the Anglo-Americans, through their knowledge of business techniques, were able to eliminate much of their Mexican-American competition.

The Santa Fe Ring, a political machine put together by Anglo-Americans with Mexican-American allies, used violence, manipulation of the land tax, and political chicanery to wrest control of most of the land grants from villagers by the 1900s. With the erosion of their landholdings, plus the Depression and the drought of the 1930s, Mexican Americans had to fall back on the welfare and employment programs of the New Deal. They lost not only their land and their independence, but their pride and their self-confidence as well.

In the Southwest during the Depression, local political leaders, welfare organizations, and law enforcement agencies repatriated large numbers of Mexican Americans to Mexico, including many who were legal residents and married to U.S. citizens. This exile and a similar roundup in the 1950s sowed permanent seeds of distrust and dislike among Mexican Americans toward American agencies.

The current distress in northern New Mexico is a result of the Mexican Americans' loss of ownership or access to the natural resources of the region that have passed into Anglo-American or U.S. government hands. Most government programs designed to reduce poverty have failed because they have struggled with the symptoms rather than addressed the fundamental cause of poverty, namely, the alienation of the Mexican-American people from the land of northern New Mexico.

In addition to their loss of land, Mexican Americans have been neglected by Anglo-American historians whose interest has focused more on the romantic periods of Spanish exploration, conquest, and settlement than on the cultural story of the Mexican-American inhabitants of the Southwest. Historians have preferred to dwell upon the westward movement of Anglo-American frontiersmen, rather than upon the problems of Mexican Americans' adjustment. Chroniclers have overlooked Mexican-American political and military leaders, explorers, pioneers, ranchers, and businessmen who played important roles in the history of the Southwest.

Language and the Arts

Many Mexican Americans are bilingual and speak Spanish not only to communicate with foreign-born relatives, but habitually and as a matter of tradition. For years the state legislature of New Mexico was officially bilingual. The right to speak Spanish was an inalienable right guaranteed to a conquered people. This symbol has gained significance because the right to speak Spanish has been suppressed by the public school system, especially in the Southwest.

In his study of the political integration of Mexican Americans, Garcia (1987) found that almost 70% have no English ability. This statistic seems to support the findings of LaBrack and Leonard (1984), who report that most Mexican-American mothers speak Spanish to their children and that Spanish is the dominant language of church activities. This further explains why many Mexican-American children have difficulty with English in school and why children must interpret for parents in business outside the home.

The constant migration across the border reinforces the presence and power of the Spanish language. As Mexican Americans are migrating eastward, many school systems and community colleges are beginning to offer instruction in English as a second language and are also experimenting with bilingual education.

The historical suppression of Spanish has tended to degrade the quality of the Spanish that is spoken. Many immigrants to the United States are illiterate agricultural workers who speak a variety of rural Spanish. Years of exposure to the dominant culture have meant that English words have been adapted to Spanish syntax.

Spanish, like any language, is more than a means of communication; it is the embodiment of a culture. As such, it offers a measure of cohesion, a reason for cooperation, a sense security, even a point of pride.

In addition to formal verbal communication, there is verbal play. Mexican Americans "rely heavily on jokes, jocular talk, and in-group humor to relieve tensions and stress caused by cultural conflicts. Jokes are an important means of communication within families and among close friends" (Castro, 1982, p. 277).

The artists of Mexico gained inspiration from the spirit of freedom and the fervent patriotism brought by the Mexican Revolution. They were inspired as well by a fresh realization of the wealth of Mexico's cultural past. The painters and sculptors avidly studied the great carvings and frescoes created in the ancient civilization of the Maya, the powerful sculptures left by the Aztecs, and the murals to be found in Mexico's many Spanish-colonial churches and shrines. The primary goal of the painters was to give birth to a new national art as noble as that of the ancient Indians.

In the 1920s the country's first major exposition of native arts and crafts was organized. The entire range of Mexico's vibrant profusion of folk art, from pottery and papier-mâché figures to ceramics and lacquerwork, were brought together. The effect inspired a new respect for the country's rich culture. The government was then persuaded to let Diego Rivera and other artists paint murals in government buildings. The painters responded to the challenges of preaching the revolutionary gospel in paint and restoring the mural to its high place in Mexican art.

The contemporary art movement is an aggressive social protest criticizing the ills of the dominant American culture and the exalted self-worth of that culture (Meier & Rivera, 1981). It also has deep roots in traditional pre-Hispanic and colonial Mexico, with some influence of American art in content and form.

Mural art depicting the Mexican-American experience in the United States can be found in many major U.S. cities, particularly in the Southwest. Mural art has two purposes: to teach history and to serve as a voice against oppression. The mural is "an art of advocacy, and in many cases it was intended to change consciousness and promote political action" (Goldman, 1982, p. 111). These murals portray such cultural experiences as violence, "progress" as viewed from the Mexican-American perspective, and the negative images of Mexican-American culture portrayed in American movies, rodeos, and art. The three most prominent muralists were Rivera, who idolized the Aztec Indians from whom Mexican Americans are descended; Jose Clemente Orozco, an *hispanista* who embraced the Spanish culture more tenaciously than his own; and David Alfaro Siqueiros, who "used indigenous motifs as allegories or metaphors for contemporary struggles" (Goldman, 1982, p. 116).

Racism and Prejudice

The problem of prejudice, as it presents itself to society, consists of overt acts that deny equal status or opportunity to people because of their racial, religious, or ethnic identity. The term *prejudice* is also used in a specialized sense to describe an individual state of mind or attitude.

Dwerkin (1964), in a study of 280 Mexican Americans in Southern California, found significant differences between Mexican Americans born in the United States and those born in Mexico, both in their stereotypes of Anglos and in their own self-images. In general, the U.S.-born Mexican Americans held more negative attitudes toward Anglos and toward themselves than did the Mexican-born. Similarly, Buriel and Vasquez (1982), assessing the stereotypes of persons of Mexican descent held by first-, second-, and third-generation Mexicans, found evidence that with each successive generation, the stereotype became more negative and more closely approximated the Anglos' stereotypes of persons of Mexican descent.

The range in skin color of Mexican Americans is from white, through mestizo and mulatto brown, to black. Darker Mexicans typically experience more prejudice and racism in their own country stemming from their descent. This factor is magnified for Mexican Americans in the United States because of the racism and prejudice in this country based on skin color (Ruiz & Padillo, 1977).

In a study by Casas and Atkinson (1981), undergraduate students at the University of California, Santa Barbara, were asked to indicate the characteristics that most people would use to describe a Mexican student. The 10 most stereotypic statements generated were as follows: poor personal hygiene habits, comes from a violent family, acts defensively when confronted, has a low GPA, does not come from a middle-class family, does not accept political opinions of others, does not use cocaine, does not plan to attend graduate school, is religious, and does not complete assignments on time.

The Mexican American is truly representative of the underclass in the dominant Anglo culture. The dominant culture wants Mexican Americans to speak English, but at the same time segregates them into barrios. Anglos expect Mexican Americans to be more like Anglo-Americans, but will not fully accept them into Anglo society because of distorted stereotypes.

Acculturation among middle-class Mexican Americans was accelerated after World War II. The rapidly expanding Mexican-American middle class sensed that acceptance depended upon an ability to speak English well, to secure a university or high school degree, to belong to the proper civic clubs, to live in houses in middle- or upper-class neighborhoods, and to maintain Anglo-American life-styles. For many, the attempt to reconcile traditional ties with present pressures led to severe emotional and personal conflicts.

Sociopolitical Factors

Mexican-American professionals entered politics to advance their careers. They were defined as approved Mexican-American leaders, but were denied the power to alter local politics. The League of United Latin Americans (LULAC) and some new, emerging Mexican-American organizations have formed to demand social and political equality. Today, LULAC has become the Mexican-

American equivalent of Rotary or Kiwanis clubs. The organization focuses on patriotic, social, and charitable programs to accelerate and to smooth Mexican-American social mobility into the American mainstream.

It was in the period following World War II that the California-born Community Service Organization (CSO) became important and meaningful. The prime objective of CSO was to get large numbers of Mexican Americans to register and vote. Two other political groups founded in the 1950s developed similar patterns of political action. The Mexican American Political Association (MAPA), founded in California in 1958, and the Political Association of Spanish Speaking Organizations (PASSO), organized in Texas, were formed to negotiate with, influence, and/or pressure the political system at the party level.

Though 1 of every 16 people in the United States is of Hispanic ancestry, in 1980 only 5 of the 435 members of the U.S. House of Representatives were Hispanic (Welch & Hibbing, 1984). Welch and Hibbing (1984) define two forms of representation: *descriptive,* in which people are represented by one from their cultural group, and *substantive,* in which the concerns of the people are represented by one outside the cultural group. Most representation of Mexican Americans is substantive, even though many districts are densely populated with Hispanics.

By far the largest numbers of organized Mexican Americans today are in the labor movement. They form a substantial part of the membership of many unions and hold many important policy-level leadership positions.

In the 1960s, many nationwide factors contributed to social unrest. Among these were the influence of the civil rights movement, the political activities of the Kennedys, the programs of President Johnson's War on Poverty, and the appearance of two Mexican-American leaders, Cesar Chavez and Reis Lopez Tijerina.

In 1968, high school students began a series of strikes that started in California and then flickered across the entire Southwest. The protest was directed, most of all, against the use of schools to Anglicize Mexican students. Out of the student movements in the late 1960s emerged the "Chicano" movement. As used by students and young people in the barrios, the term *Chicano* refers to an individual committed to the Chicano movement. In general, the term is associated with the physical and spiritual liberation of the Mexican-American people from poverty, welfare, unemployment, a self-image of inferiority, and Anglo-American dominance.

The first urban upheavals to involve Mexican Americans were the Los Angeles riots of the early 1970s. Representatives from almost every major Mexican-American organization in the United States came to march, protest, fraternize, and discuss the disproportionately high rates at which Mexican Americans were drafted into the army and killed or wounded in Vietnam. Mexican Americans found themselves charged, beaten, and jailed by members of the Los Angeles Sheriff's Department. The indignation was heightened by the murder, by deputies, of Ruben Salazar, the most prominent Mexican-American journalist in the United States. Out of these events emerged barrio community organizations. The barrio organizations are committed to the improvement of communities through planned programs in housing, economic development, health services, social services, youth programs, human resources development, and education.

Child-Rearing Practices

During the years when children are young, the Mexican-American home is usually child centered. Both parents tend to be permissive and indulgent with the younger children. Panitz, McConchie, Sauber, and Fonseca (1983) have observed that "the male child is overindulged and accorded greater status than the female" (p. 37). Children receive training in responsibility by being assigned tasks or responsibilities according to their age and ability. Much of children's self-esteem is related to how well they and others perceive them to be carrying out assigned family responsibilities.

Differences in patterns of behavior between male and female children are taught implicitly and explicitly from infancy. The male is taught how to think and act like a man and the female is taught her feminine role. At the onset of adolescence, the difference in patterns of behavior between boys and girls becomes even more markedly apparent. The female is likely to remain much closer to home, and to be protected and guarded in her contact with others beyond the family. Through her relationships with her mother and other female relatives she is prepared for the role of wife and mother. On the other hand, the adolescent male, following the model of his father, is given much more freedom to come and go as he chooses and is encouraged to gain much worldly knowledge and experience outside the home in preparation for the time when he will assume the role of husband and father (Mirandé, 1985).

Religious Practices

With the immigration of Mexicans, the Catholic church began the building of parochial schools and the Americanization of the Mexican population. Both of these motives were inspired, to a large extent, by the desire to defend Mexican Americans against Protestant missionaries and to keep Mexican youth from entering a public school system that was at least latently anti-Catholic and publicly devoted to secular values.

Oppression within the structure of the church extended beyond under-representation in the power structure of the church. The Catholic church in the United States viewed Mexican-American Catholicism as weak and without commitment to faith (Mirandé, 1985). In an attempt to "Americanize" the church, an attempt was made to "Americanize" the Mexican American. For example, masses were not offered in Spanish and the Catholic schools did not offer bilingual education.

With the shift in social position after World War II, the Mexican-American tie to Catholicism was loosened as many began to join Protestant denominations. The Pentecostals especially gained ground among both urban workers and rural villagers.

The church and faith have a central role in Mexican-American culture. As Mexican Americans are settling into smaller communities, they are beginning to establish their own churches. Mexican-American worship services are sometimes less formal than those in the dominant culture, incorporating the music of guitars, accordions, maracas, tambourines, and bongo drums.

In addition to participation in the Catholic Mass, many Mexican-American women keep home altars. These altars are "distinctive because they represent a personal, private, and most importantly, a creative source of religious experience" (Turner, 1982, p. 309). Objects typically seen on home altars include representations of the Virgin Mary and the Great Mother of Mexico, the Sacred Heart, and Jesus. According to Turner (1982), the presence of body images "is an indication of the essential desire to bring spiritual and physical, social and profane realms together" (p. 318). Candles symbolize the light of faith, the active acknowledgment of the relationship between the human and the divine. Photographs and statues of political figures also grace these altars. The pictures and statues represent many relationships, and the women who build them are compared to the Virgin Mary, prayerfully interceding for those represented.

Although levels of religious belief, commitment, and actual practice vary greatly among Mexican Americans, it does appear that Catholicism historically has had and still has a powerful influence on the lives of Mexican Americans.

Family Structure and Dynamics

There is no single Mexican-American family pattern based on one unique traditional culture. There are literally millions of Mexican-American families, all differing significantly from one another along a variety of dimensions. There are significant regional, historical, political, socioeconomic, acculturation, and assimilation factors that result in a multitude of family patterns of living and of coping with each other and with the Anglo environment (Mirandé, 1985).

Among Mexican Americans, the family is the core of thinking and behavior, and the center from which the view of the world extends. Even with respect to identification, the Mexican-American self-identity is likely to take second place to the family.

A Mexican American in need of emotional support, guidance, food, or money expects and is expected to turn to family first to meet such needs. A Mexican American may seek help from others only when there is absolutely no other alternative. The strength of the family in providing security to its members is sometimes expressed through a sharing of material things with other relatives even when there is precious little to meet one's own immediate needs.

Due to the patriarchal nature of the culture, relatives on the father's side of the family may be considered more important than those from the mother's side. Among extended family members there is often much communication, visiting, sharing, and closeness. It is possible that a family may sever all relations with one of its members if that individual, through personal behavior, brings shame or dishonor to the family.

The husband and father is the autocratic head of the household. He tends to remain aloof and independent from the rest of the family. All family members are expected to be respectful of him and to accede to his will or direction. Should he misuse his authority in the family, he will lose respect within the community (Panitz et al., 1983).

In relating to his children, the father frequently serves as disciplinarian. During the children's earlier years, the father is often permissive, warm, and close to them. This changes significantly as each child reaches the onset of puberty. At this time, the father's behavior toward his children becomes much more reserved, authoritarian, and demanding of respect.

An understanding of the concept of *machismo* is important to an understanding of the use of authority in the family. Mirandé (1988) identifies the positive aspects of machismo as bravery, courage, self-defense, responsibility, respect, altruism, pride, protection, steadfastness, individualism, androgyny, and honor.

The wife and mother is supposed to be completely devoted to her husband and children. Her role is to serve the needs of her husband, support his actions and decisions, and take care of the home and children.

Mexican Americans use an extended family structure that includes godparents (*compradazgo*) who ensure the welfare and religious education of the children. Choosing the proper godparents is essential, because it "link[s] the families through the child" (LaBrack & Leonard, 1984, p. 531). Traditional godparents assume serious obligations toward their godchildren and take them into their own households whenever necessary. By extension, godparents become honorary family members. Like the traditional family, the choosing of godparents has been declining, particularly in cities where pressures on Mexican Americans to acculturate are greater and where the dynamics of urban life dilute traditional practices.

Cultural Values and Attitudes

Current historical evidence emphasizes the cultural variation among Mexican Americans across time and geographic areas. For the Mexican American, material objects are usually necessities and not ends in themselves. Work is viewed as a necessity for survival, but not as a value in itself. Much higher value is assigned to other life activities in the Mexican culture. It is through physical and mental well-being and through an ability to experience, in response to environment, emotional feelings and to express these to one another and share these, that one experiences the greatest rewards and satisfactions in life. It is much more valuable to experience things directly, through intellectual awareness and emotional involvement, than indirectly, through remembering past accomplishments or accumulating wealth. The philosopher, poet, musician, and artist are more often revered in this culture than the businessman or financier.

Mexican Americans are likely to live and experience life most completely in the present. For an individual from the lower socioeconomic portion of the society, a limited time orientation may result from immediate survival needs. Another factor contributing to this orientation may stem from the influence of an old Native American cultural belief in the concept of the "limited good." In effect, this is the belief that there is only so much good in the world and, therefore, only so much good is possible in any one person's life. It matters not how industrious one is, for one will get no more than one's share of good during a lifetime.

In the dominant culture of the United States, being responsible is equated with being punctual. The Mexican-American concept of responsibility is based on other values, such as attending to the immediate needs of family or friends, and thus Mexican Americans do not place much value on, and may be casual about, punctuality.

Whereas members of the dominant culture of the United States are taught to value openness, frankness, and directness, the traditional Mexican-American approach requires the use of much diplomacy and tact when communicating with another individual. Concern and respect for the feelings of others dictate that a screen be provided behind which an individual may preserve dignity. A great deal of faith is placed in family and friends, such that lasting relationships are developed. Goals do not lie in the accumulation of material goods, but in the good that can be done for all people.

The manner of expression is likely to be elaborate and indirect, since the aim is to make the personal relationship at least appear harmonious, to show respect for the other's individuality. To the Mexican American, direct argument or contradiction appears rude and disrespectful. On the surface one may seem agreeable, manners dictating that one not reveal genuine opinions openly, unless one knows the other well and unless there is time to differ tactfully. This concept of courtesy often causes misunderstandings between Anglos and Mexican Americans.

Mexican Americans experience a high degree of sensitivity to the environment. They use the full range of physiological senses to experience the world around them. Thus they are more likely than Anglos to want to touch, taste, smell, feel, or be close to an object or person on which their attention is focused.

Implications

Mexican Americans are present-time oriented, and teachers and counselors should bear this in mind when working with Mexican-American clients to set concrete, short-term goals. Mexican Americans also value the appearance of agreeability; they consider disagreeability to be rude. Helping professionals need to understand that it can be most constructive to be indirect with Mexican Americans, as this is their custom until they get to know an individual.

Clearly, helpers who are aware of the Mexican-American culture will be less likely to say or do something that will offend Mexican-American clients or make them less receptive to counseling. In an agency setting, helping professionals can work to break down any stereotypes they may hold about Mexican Americans by speaking with other professionals who are in contact with Mexican Americans and by reading about the culture of this group. Service agencies need to be aware of the migration of Mexican Americans into their communities and to learn about issues that concern them. Agency professionals need to confront their own prejudices and break down any beliefs they have that the Anglo way is the only way.

More culturally relevant educational programs are needed for Mexican Americans. Educators aware of the Mexican-American value system may wish to greet students or clients as soon as they arrive, acknowledging the importance of *personalismo.* The sensitive educator or counselor will use first names with Mexican Americans and will introduce him- or herself by first name. The aware helper will understand that direct eye contact with an older Mexican American may communicate a lack of respect.

Because of potential differences in the perception of time, educators or counselors should make appointments with Mexican Americans immediately rather than several weeks in advance. A directive approach is likely to be more useful than a nondirective approach to issues or problems.

Helpers must realize that Mexican Americans come from such diverse backgrounds and cultures that they cannot be classified based solely on the ability to speak either English or Spanish. The helper must understand that regional differences and differences based on the degree of acculturation into the dominant Anglo culture have major implications for understanding Mexican Americans. The goal of understanding Mexican Americans is to help them find a place in relation to tradition and to feel comfortable in moving between the traditions of the Mexican culture and the traditions of the culture of the United States. Thus the Mexican American becomes able to function and to understand the meaning of being bicultural.

Questions for Review and Reflection

(1) The Mexican-American population is the fastest growing in the United States. What influence will this growth have on your role as an educator or counselor?

(2) Distinguish among the terms *Chicano, Hispanic,* and *Mexican American.* What difference, if any, exists in the degree of acculturation between individuals who use different labels to describe the same ethnic group?

(3) What is machismo? How does it influence Mexican Americans' interactions within their own culture, with the dominant culture, and with other culturally different groups?

(4) What political organization has been most influential for Mexican Americans? Why has it been so influential?

(5) What event in the history of Mexican Americans has influenced the dominant culture most in its acceptance of Mexican Americans? Why?

(6) How can educators or counselors intervene with Mexican Americans who view family as the primary source of support?

(7) What is the impact of Standard English fluency on Mexican Americans? How should educators or counselors approach students or clients who view Spanish as their primary language?

(8) What are the unique characteristics of the Mexican-American culture? What major problems confront Mexicans coming to the United States? How do these factors influence educational and counseling practices?

(9) Distinguish among traditional, atraditional, and duotraditional Mexican Americans. What strategies and techniques should educators and counselors use with each group?

(10) What influence do assumptions regarding Mexican-American poverty (for instance, as presented by Stout, 1980) have on educational or counseling programs developed for Mexican Americans?

References

Alvarez, R. (1973). The psycho-historical and socioeconomic development of the Chicano community in the United States. *Social Science Quarterly, 53,* 920-942.

Arias, M. B. (1986). The context of education for Hispanic students: An overview. *American Journal of Education, 95,* 26-57.

Buriel, R., & Vasquez, R. (1982). Stereotypes of Mexican descent persons: Attitudes of three generations of Mexican American and Anglo-American adolescents. *Journal of Cross-Cultural Psychology, 13,* 59-70.

Casas, J. M., & Atkinson, D. R. (1981). The Mexican American in higher education: An example of subtle stereotyping. *Personnel and Guidance Journal, 59,* 473-476.

Castro, R. (1982). Mexican American women's sexual jokes. *Aztlan, 13,* 275-293.

Church, G. (1985, July 8). Hispanics: A melding of cultures. *Time,* p. 36.

Duran, L. I., & Bernard, H. R. (Eds.). (1973). *Introduction to Chicano studies.* New York: Macmillan.

Dwerkin, A. G. (1964). Stereotypes and self-images by native-born and foreign-born Mexican-Americans. *Sociology and Social Research, 49,* 214-224.

Garcia, J. A. (1987). The political integration of Mexican immigrants: Examining some political orientations. *International Migration Review, 21,* 372-389.

Goldman, S. M. (1982). Mexican muralism: Its social-educative roles in Latin America and the United States. *Aztlan, 13,* 111-133.

Hernandez, L., & Carlquist-Hernandez, K. (1979). Humanization of the counseling-teaching process for Latinos: Learning principles. *Journal of Non-White Concerns, 7,* 150-158.

Hurtado, A., & Arce, C. H. (1987). Mexicans, Chicanos, Mexican Americans, or Pochos: ¿Qué somos? The impact of language and nativity on ethnic labeling. *Aztlan, 17,* 103-130.

Kiskadden, R. W., & Rossell, N. H. (1979). *Mexican American studies: An instructional bulletin.* Los Angeles: Los Angeles Unified School District.

LaBrack, B., & Leonard, K. (1984). Conflict and compatibility in Punjabi-Mexican immigrant families in rural California. *Journal of Marriage, 46,* 527-537.

Matute-Bianchi, M. E. (1986). Ethnic identities and patterns of school success and failure among Mexican-descent and Japanese-American students in a California high school: An ethnographic analysis. *American Journal of Education, 95,* 233-255.

Meier, M. S., & Rivera, F. (1981). *Dictionary of Mexican American experience.* Westport, CT: Greenwood.

Miller, S., Nicolau, S., Orr, M., Valdivieso, R., & Walker, G. (1988). *Too late to patch: Reconsidering opportunities for Hispanic and other dropouts.* Washington, DC: Hispanic Policy Development Project.

Mirandé, A. (1985). *The Chicano experience: An alternative perspective.* Notre Dame, IN: University of Notre Dame Press.

Mirandé, A. (1988). Qué gaucho es ser macho: It's a drag to be a macho man. *Aztlan, 17,* 63-89.

Ortego, P. D. (1973). The Chicano renaissance. In L. I. Duran & H. R. Bernard (Eds.), *Introduction to Chicano studies* (pp. 331-349). New York: Macmillan.

Panitz, D. R., McConchie, R. D., Sauber, S. R., & Fonseca, J. A. (1983). The role of machismo and the Hispanic family in the etiology and treatment of alcoholism in Hispanic American males. *American Journal of Family Therapy, 11,* 31-44.

Ruiz, R. A., & Padillo, A. M. (1977). Counseling Latinos. *Personnel and Guidance Journal, 55,* 401-408.

Stout, R. J. (1980). No future: The life of the migrant child. *American Education, 4,* 24-29.

Turner, K. F. (1982). Mexican American home altars: Towards their interpretation. *Aztlan, 13,* 309-326.

Welch, S., & Hibbing, J. R. (1984). Hispanic representation in the U.S. Congress. *Social Science Quarterly, 65,* 328-335.

10

Puerto Rican Americans

Puerto Rican Americans are the only migrants who have come to the mainland of the United States as citizens of this country, with the rights of naturalized citizens. Even with these rights, Puerto Ricans are an extremely devalued group. The basis of this devaluation is racial prejudice and a language barrier.

The island of Borinquen, renamed Puerto Rico by the Spanish, is characterized as a mixture of cultural influences, marked by vestiges of the Taino Indians who first inhabited the island, by more than 500 years of Spanish colonialism, and by more than three-quarters of a century of domination by the United States. The Spanish influence, with its system of feudal agriculture, the Roman Catholic church, language, and civil law, remained dominant in Puerto Rican culture until the turn of the century.

New economic changes developed for Puerto Ricans late in the nineteenth century, when the island came into the possession of the United States. The feudal hacienda owners were supplanted by U.S. corporate interests. Until 1932, the federal government maintained a relaxed attitude toward the economy of Puerto Rico, with the result that most of the investment and development in Puerto Rico came from private U.S. capital. Montijo (1985) concludes that "by retaining Puerto Rico as an unincorporated territory and imposing its citizenship on Puerto Ricans, the United States greatly contributed to what could be described as Puerto Rico's national identity crisis" (p. 436).

Under Governor Luis Muñoz Marín, Puerto Rico implemented Operation Bootstrap, a development program designed to raise the standard of living on the island. In 20 years of effort, the Puerto Rican government raised the per capita income by more than 300%, and by 1960 some 600 new factories had been established, creating an estimated 45,000 new jobs. Moreover, the government aided in the training of personnel by building factories for rent at attractive rates and through various tax incentives (Rosado, 1986).

Puerto Ricans have benefited individually from the government monies invested in roads, housing, education, health, and welfare. Even so, by 1972, the per capita income was only $1,713, nearly $300 behind the 30-year prediction of Operation Bootstrap. Moreover, an urban, consumer-based middle class had developed with enough political power to oppose increases in the minimum wage standard, with the result that the distribution of income across the island became increasingly skewed (Lopez & Petras, 1974).

Increased economic and cultural penetration from the United States, displacement of the rural farm community, the creation of an urban underclass as a result of the decline in agriculture, and the lure of U.S. culture all contributed to the heavy Puerto Rican migration to the continental United States. A Puerto Rican American can be described as anyone who had at least one parent born in that territory, and those residing in the United States can be described as members of four subgroups: (a) individuals born in the United States who live in New York City, referred to as "Nuyoricans," (b) those born in the United States who live in places other than New York City, (c) those born on the island of Puerto Rico who live in New York City, and (d) those born in Puerto Rico who live elsewhere in the United States (Lopez & Petras, 1974).

By 1980 there were nearly 2.2 million first- and second-generation Puerto Ricans living in the continental United States. Although New York City remains the area of heaviest concentration, Puerto Ricans have moved to other parts of the country (U.S. Department of Commerce, Bureau of the Census, 1980). Fitzpatrick (1987) reports that the Puerto Rican population in the United States is becoming more of a second- and third-generation group. In 1970, 58.4% of Puerto Ricans living in New York were born in Puerto Rico; by 1980, that figure was only 42%.

Acculturation

Puerto Ricans are hardworking people who are inculcated with fundamental Catholic ideology. Likewise, a strong sense of self-worth and the concept of personal dignity (*dignidad*), both as an ideal and as a defense, has helped Puerto Rican Americans maintain a sense of community and personal pride despite oppressive socioeconomic conditions. Another factor that has contributed positively to the resilience of the Puerto Rican community is a need for interaction with others; no great need for privacy exists in Puerto Rican culture. Another sustaining characteristic is the emphasis on spiritual and human values rather than on the commercial values of the United States. This last feature has endowed Puerto Rican communities with a flexibility and a source of inner strength in the face of economic hardships.

Adjustments to life in the United States have been eased by the fact that Puerto Ricans are already familiar with public education standards, wage systems, large hospitals, mass communication, and the electoral process. This gives them an advantage over other Hispanic migrant groups, who may not have experienced these key structures.

One of the most overt issues of acculturation for Puerto Rican Americans has been language. Employers complain of a labor force with which they cannot communicate. Employment services are reluctant to place workers with little fluency in English. In addition, problems in schools are acute, because many Puerto Rican children enter the public school system with little English proficiency.

There is a fear of the loss of identity as a Puerto Rican with the loss of the Spanish language. However, Puerto Ricans are realistic about the need to master the English language and to adjust to patterns of living in the dominant culture of the United States. Fitzpatrick (1987) suggests that the majority of Puerto Ricans are striving to become bicultural in that they "do not see any form of separatism as either practically possible or socially desirable. But they seek a form of life in which, as New Yorkers, they remain decidedly themselves" (p. 7).

Because the family unit is so important to Puerto Ricans, some adjustments are required by assimilation. For instance, consensual marriage is not recognized in the United States, and in many states common-law marriage has been outlawed. The mother of children born in a consensual arrangement is ineligible for benefits that might be afforded a widow, abandoned, or divorced parent. Moreover, the custom of early marriage conflicts with many age-of-consent laws.

Unfortunately, the problems of acculturation are more difficult for younger Puerto Ricans who have grown up in low-income Puerto Rican urban communities in the United States. Children learn the dominant cultural norms in school, and this can result in a devaluing of the Puerto Rican culture in favor of Anglo norms. In addition, the media often portray Puerto Ricans in a negative manner. This lack of a strong sense of cultural identity, compounded by the racial ambiguity faced by the new generation of Puerto Rican Americans, results in conflict between the dominant culture and Puerto Rican culture. Lacking many of the characteristics of traditional Puerto Rican culture that facilitated the adaptability of first-generation immigrants, later generations of Puerto Rican Americans face real problems of identity as they assimilate.

Being forced to cope with their indigenous culture and the dominant culture of the United States simultaneously frequently generates a high degree of stress. Despite the numerous barriers, many Puerto Rican Americans acculturate well, adopting the cultural elements of the dominant society. Other Puerto Ricans cope by attempting to balance elements of both cultures, or they refuse to adopt the dominant culture of the United States.

Poverty and Economic Concerns

Poverty and a lack of opportunity on the island of Puerto Rico are two of the primary reasons that Puerto Ricans migrate to the U.S. mainland. Chenault (1970) reports that about 70% of all Puerto Ricans who move to New York City settle in Harlem and the navy yard districts. This migration to the slum areas exemplifies the very low economic status of the migrant Puerto Ricans.

The U.S. Bureau of Census (1980) reports that 30-33% of Puerto Rican Americans live in poverty. This is in contrast to 10-12% of all U.S. citizens. Puerto Rican Americans also had the lowest median family income of the Hispanic subgroups in 1980. The median family income for Puerto Ricans was $9,900, while for Mexican Americans it was $15,200 and for Cuban Americans, $17,500.

Other factors related to poverty show Puerto Rican Americans to be behind the general U.S. population. For instance, the dropout rate for Puerto Ricans in 1984 was reported at 60% (Fitzpatrick, 1987). Failure to complete high school, coupled with a decrease in the number of available blue-collar jobs, has resulted in a 40-45% unemployment rate for Puerto Rican youth (16-24 years old), compared with a rate of 23% for Anglo-American youth in the same age group (U.S. Department of Commerce, Bureau of the Census, 1980). Rodriguez (1989) reports that the poverty rate among Puerto Ricans is higher than that for Caucasians, African Americans, and other Hispanic groups.

History of Oppression

Oppressive conditions are not new to Puerto Ricans, who have experienced a history of oppression from external powers for the last 400 years. The original settlers of the island of Puerto Rico were the Taino Indians, who were forced to defend their land against the Carib Indians and, later, the Spanish. In 1508, the arrival of Ponce de Leon signaled the beginning of official colonization and rule of Puerto Rico by the Spanish empire. The Taino soon realized that they were enslaved by the Spaniards, whose primary needs were to exploit the land and use them as a source of cheap labor. The Spanish ruled Puerto Rico until 1897, when the island was granted autonomy. The island was later attacked 26 times by foreign countries and finally ceded to the United States, the twenty-sixth attacker. Thus Puerto Rico continued as a colony of a foreign power. After two years of military occupation, the U.S. Congress provided Puerto Rico with a territorial form of government (Cardona, 1974).

In the United States, Puerto Rican Americans form a large part of New York's unskilled labor force and have found employment readily in the lowest-paying jobs. Discrimination at these lower levels of the occupational structure appears to be related to factors of language difference, practices of union discrimination, and monopolies on certain jobs that have traditionally been held and guarded by other ethnic groups. Moreover, certain professional agencies have refused to recognize licenses and training sanctioned in Puerto Rico, making it difficult for skilled Puerto Ricans living in the continental United States to find equivalent work (Lopez & Petras, 1974).

Unemployment among Puerto Rican males continues to be approximately twice that of the general population. Unemployment among Puerto Rican females, though higher than that for males, is much nearer the national norm. Median family incomes have historically been lower than those of either Mexican-American or Cuban-American families.

Language and the Arts

Most Puerto Ricans consider Spanish their native tongue, and about three out of every four Puerto Rican Americans report that Spanish is the language spoken in the home. Because Spanish is the native tongue of most Puerto Rican Americans, its usage has increased greatly in the communities where migrants reside. These Spanish-speaking areas provide a link to Puerto Rico as well as help the recent migrant with the adjustment to the mainland. The shared language is one of the major ways of preserving the Puerto Rican culture in a new environment (Wagenheim, 1975).

According to Fitzpatrick (1987), there is an increasing awareness of the value of bilingualism among Puerto Rican Americans. However, school systems have had difficulty in implementing bilingual programs. Questions center around how to teach English as a second language and how to assist children with a mastery of both English and Spanish. As a result of a court case in 1974 brought by the Aspira organization, the Board of Education of the City of New York is required to provide bilingual instruction for Puerto Rican students. Even so, 10 years later "only 30 percent of entitled students receive the full bilingual education that is prescribed by law" (Fitzpatrick, 1987, p. 168).

Puerto Ricans have long been famous for their lively and expressive folk art and music, which is evidence of their gusto for life and their high energy. The nineteenth century is considered the Puerto Rican Golden Age of literary, musical, and artistic works. From 1898 to 1920, Puerto Rican authors were primarily concerned with clinging to their past heritage. This literature provides an understanding of the struggles and dreams of those trying to adjust to their country's being a possession of the United States (Cardona, 1974).

Quero-Chiesa (1974) notes that the Puerto Rican author in the United States has to face a cultural conflict "so serious that it becomes a matter of life and death to him as an artist. Before him rises the wall of the English language, isolating him from the American literary life" (p. 64). Not only is the language a barrier to the writer, but the change in cultural values from honor, romanticism, the Latin sense of family unity, and the hierarchy of intellectual life to pragmatism creates confusion in the minds of writers that is reflected in their work. Thus for the Puerto Rican-American author, the Hispanic culture is a source from which to draw inspiration. To capture themes for their writing,

> frequently they latch on to some native motif, such as liberty, folklore or popular typology. This kind of literature about the idealized motherland with its romantic-nationalistic accent is usually provincial in character and often embodies chauvinism and an exultation of the picturesque. (Quero-Chiesa, 1974, p. 65)

Along with literary works, music, and accomplishments on the stage, in films, and on television, the Puerto Ricans have a folk art, *santeria,* which began in the sixteenth century. Vice (1974) reports that the "santeros carved wooden saints for their religious ceremonies and beliefs, and for a very long time, every home had either a set of the Three Kings or some statuette" (p. 144). The *santeros* are generally country folk with little or no training or formal education, but with a distinct talent for carving.

Racism and Prejudice

Puerto Ricans did not experience much discrimination based on race until they came to the United States. Prejudice in Puerto Rico was based on class rather than race; people were excluded from social participation not because of color but because of class. Consequently, an upper-class person's behavior toward a person of color depended not on the person's color, but on his or her class position.

According to Fitzpatrick (1987), nothing is as complicated for Puerto Rican Americans in their effort to adjust to the dominant culture as is the problem of color. They represent the first group ever to come to the United States in large numbers with a tradition of widespread intermingling and intermarriage of people of different color. This blend comes from a mix of Spanish, Taino Indian, and African. The population today ranges from Caucasoid to completely Negroid, with many variations in between. On the U.S. mainland, Puerto Ricans are often expected to fit into racial categories based on color. This categorization has little meaning for Puerto Rican migrants, and can be confusing. On the island, Puerto Rican people recognize several racial categories, such as *blanco* (white), *prieto* (dark skinned), *negro* (black), and *trigueño* (tan) (Banks, 1987). Puerto Rican Americans who are intermediate in skin color do not fit neatly in a black/white classification system and are often alienated from both of these two racial groups.

Mainland attitudes have been ambivalent regarding the racial identity of Puerto Ricans. Puerto Ricans who came to the United States before World War II, and who settled in urban areas, were often ostracized by their Italian counterparts, while African-American ghetto youth were more accepting. During World War II, army camps on the island segregated Puerto Rican troops, and the U.S. Navy refused to enlist Puerto Ricans. Unless very dark and with Negroid features, Puerto Ricans were listed as white in New York City. The proportion of "colored" in Puerto Rican populations dropped with each census (Cordasco, 1973). The 1980 census identifies first- and second-generation Puerto Ricans in the United States as "Puerto Rican" (U.S. Department of Commerce, Bureau of the Census, 1980).

Sociopolitical Factors

In 1947, Puerto Ricans were granted the right to elect their own governor. Shortly thereafter, their first governor, Luis Muñoz Marín, instituted a political status called the Free Associated State of Puerto Rico. This gave more autonomy to the island and established a relationship with the United States that is similar to commonwealth status (Sociological Resources for the Social Studies, 1974).

Puerto Rico's civil status remains controversial today. There are some proponents of statehood and there other factions who argue for complete independence. Those on both sides of this argument believe that their preferred status will strengthen Puerto Rico's cultural identity and political/economic security. The status issues have implications for Puerto Ricans living on the mainland because the communities in Puerto Rico and on the mainland are integrally bound by family ties and a history of migration patterns.

Puerto Ricans are U.S. citizens naturalized by annexation, giving them the right to vote in elections, as well as making them eligible to serve in the military. Puerto Rican-American political strength has been weak in the past because election ballots have traditionally been only in English. In 1969, the Spanish-American Action Committee (SAAC) was formed to further Puerto Ricans' socioeconomic development. This organization "provides services in the areas of housing, employment, education, and community organization. In addition to providing services, SAAC also puts pressure on city officials to get them to respond to the needs of Puerto Ricans" (Cardona, 1974, p. 62). In the political arena, there is a high voter registration, but "greater political enlightenment of the Puerto Rican community has been hampered by the continuous gerrymandering of several districts with high concentrations of Puerto Ricans" (Cardona, 1974, p. 63). Fitzpatrick (1987) reports that even though Puerto Ricans are participants in a wide range of community organizations and social service programs, they are "still underrepresented in the critical area of the political process, registration and voting. As a result, political representation is low and political influence is weak" (p. 13). In some parts of the country, Puerto Rican Americans are still very weak politically, but the Puerto Rican community is growing, learning, and developing the tools to work within the political process.

Child-Rearing Practices

Puerto Ricans demonstrate a strong feeling of love for their children. Obedience and respect for parental authority are stressed in traditional Puerto Rican families. Children are not allowed to question or challenge their parents. First-generation parents do not assign rights to children; they make most decisions for their children (Juarez, 1985). Humility is a highly valued expectation, and children lower their eyes and heads to show respect for their parents. Corporal punishment, if not excessive, is accepted as a disciplinary approach. Simpson and Yinger (1972) point out that more "modern" families, usually second and third generations, have different parenting styles, believing that fewer restrictions should be placed on children. The father is still the authority figure, but his authority is more flexible and less imposing.

Boys are given greater independence and, to a great extent, left to raise themselves. Girls are carefully watched and protected. Simpson and Yinger (1972) suggest that Puerto Rican boys may find friends on the streets who are bad influences, may learn to be disrespectful and disobedient to their parents, and may even get involved with drug addiction and crime.

Compadres are special friends or favorite relatives who act as coparents. Coparents are expected to give and to receive strong loyalty, affection, respect, and services. It is not unusual for families to add nephews, nieces, godchildren, and children of a husband's extramarital alliances to the extended family.

Religious Practices

Puerto Rico is generally thought of as a Catholic nation, but the Catholicism of Puerto Ricans is unique. According to Old World criteria, Puerto Rican Catholicism was of inferior intellectual formation, with undue amounts of superstition in popular devotion (Stevens-Arroyo, 1974). Due to Spanish imperialism, Catholicism was a religion of the town, isolating the people in the hill country from the parish priest. Protestantism was introduced with the American invasion, but the Puerto Rican custom of wearing religious medals was considered incompatible with this new religion. The great devotion to the rosary and the cult of the Virgin Mary created a cultural form called *rosaria contao* (Stevens-Arroyo, 1974, p. 120).

Pentecostalism became the largest and fastest growing of Puerto Rican religions, because the importance it places on religious experience reinforced the Puerto Rican desire for intimacy with the supernatural. After migrating to New York, many Puerto Ricans found that Pentecostalism provided a means of escape from the cultural and social aimlessness they experienced in the transition from rural to city life. Nuyoricans continue "to be faithful to religious customs such as baptism and the practice of the asabache, which is a black piece of wood, usually in the shape of an arm, meant to protect the child from the evil eye" (Stevens-Arroyo, 1974, p. 128).

Puerto Rican clergy among the Protestant churches are a visible and powerful force in most civic associations and events. The abundance of Puerto Ricans in the clergy is significant evidence of the vitality of the Protestant churches, and an advantage not shared by the Catholic church.

Another form of religious practice is spiritualism, or the practice of communication with spiritual forces. It is "rooted in the belief that persons in this world can establish contact with the spirit world and can use this power to influence the spirits, either restraining the unfavorable action of evil spirits or effecting the favorable action of good spirits" (Fitzpatrick, 1987, p. 127). Spiritualist activities are conducted by a medium, a person who claims power to contact the spirit world. Believers in spiritualism also participate in folk practices that have to do with curing illnesses. In the barrio there is usually a *botanica* where herbs, potions, prayers, and "voodoo dolls" are sold.

Family Structure and Dynamics

As in most cultures of the world, the individual in Puerto Rico has a deep commitment to membership in the family. The world to a Puerto Rican consists of a pattern of intimate personal relationships, and the basic relationships are those of family. Fitzpatrick (1987) identifies a fourfold structural typology among Puerto Rican families. First, they have extended family systems, where there are strong bonds and frequent interaction among a wide range of natural or ritual kin, providing a source of strength and support. Next is the nuclear family, consisting of the mother, father, and children not living close to relatives and having weak bonds to the extended family. The third is father, mother, their children, and children of any other union or unions of husband or wife. Finally, there is the mother-based family, with children of one or more fathers, but with no permanent male in the home.

As an alternative to marriage, the consensual union is allowed. This is a relatively stable union of a man and a woman who have never gone through a religious or civil marriage ceremony, but who live together and rear a family. The number of these unions is steadily decreasing among Puerto Rican Americans. The father is required by law to recognize his children whether he lives with the mother or not. This gives the child a number of rights before the law, including the right to use the father's name, the right to support, and some rights of inheritance (Fitzpatrick, 1987).

A Puerto Rican's confidence, sense of security, and identity are closely tied to relationships in the family. The use of names is an example. A Puerto Rican generally uses the name of his or her father's father and his or her mother's father. In the case of Jose Garcia Lopez, Garcia comes from Jose's father's family name and Lopez is his mother's father's name. The wife's name in this marriage is Maria Gonzalez de Garcia. She keeps her father's father's name, Gonzalez, and adopts her husband's first family name, usually with a *de* (of) (Sociological Resources for the Social Studies, 1974).

The importance of the Puerto Rican-American extended family is evidenced in the celebration of holidays such as *Noche Buena* ("the good night," Christmas Eve), when the family gathers with close friends to celebrate. A feeling of relaxation, of caring, and of temporary retreat from problems is coupled with a feast featuring such foods as yellow rice, pigeon peas, and roast pork (Rodriguez, 1989).

Cultural Values and Attitudes

In many respects, Puerto Ricans share the heritage of the Spanish tradition in their interactions, retention of the language, fundamental Catholic theology, acceptance of class structure, hospitality, gregarious family patterns, machismo, and emphasis on the spiritual and human values of society. Banks (1987) identifies the following characteristics of Puerto Rican-American values and attitudes: interdependence, group centrality, cooperation, dignity, respect of persons, comfort with human contact, and the need of the presence of human voices to feel at ease.

One of the more obvious value shifts currently taking place among Puerto Rican Americans is the change in roles of males and females, with females becoming more independent. A shift is also occurring in the role of the child, with children beginning to behave according to dominant cultural standards of self-reliance, aggressiveness, competitiveness, inquisitiveness, and independence. These behaviors are considered disrespectful by Puerto Rican-American parents who are accustomed to more submissive children. Further, migration to the U.S. mainland has weakened extended kinship bonds, causing the family to find itself alienated in the dominant culture.

Many of the Puerto Rican values continue, such as personalism, which is a form of individualism that focuses on the inner importance of the person, and the role of the *padrino,* a person of influence who helps the Puerto Rican. This role is often operationalized through the personal relationships developed through business affairs. Puerto Rican Americans are quite sensitive to personal insult. They also have a sense of destiny and a sense of a hierarchical world. Thus Puerto Rican-American individuals are greatly influenced by the family and the community and have been influenced by the dominant culture of the United States. The family and community bonds of Puerto Rican Americans contrasts with the dominant culture, which is oriented mostly around the individual and his or her accomplishments.

The dominant culture also has a different value of time, in that it encourages planning for the future and requires a compulsive time orientation instead of living for today and having an extended time orientation. Thus the Puerto Rican orientation toward time causes problems in the dominant culture and often leads to loss of employment on the basis of a different value orientation.

Implications

The unique nature of the Puerto Rican migration and of Puerto Rican experiences provide an opportunity to make generalizations about multiethnic curriculum concepts. Banks (1987) identifies three key concepts specific to Puerto Rican-American experiences—cultural conflict, racial problems, and colonialism—and suggests strategies for incorporating them into the curriculum. Cultural conflict involves the many problems Puerto Ricans experience when they encounter new norms, values, and roles on the mainland. Discussions about family case studies can help students understand the adjustment problems of Puerto Ricans. The concept of racial problems can provide an opportunity to learn about the racial complexity of Puerto Ricans and related identity problems. Teaching activities for this concept can have the value of increasing sensitivity to racial problems of other ethnic groups as well as understanding Puerto Ricans' concerns. Colonialism can be covered by stressing the consequences of control by foreign powers, such as rebellions, political ambiguity, and instability on the island. Another goal for teaching this concept is to generalize the effects of oppression to other ethnic groups. All of these concepts can assist students in thinking about their role in making decisions and taking action to help eliminate problems of racism, poverty, and political powerlessness.

Inclan (1985) reminds us that principles of psychoanalytical theory have limited value with poor Hispanic people. There was once an expectation that psychoanalytical practice had promise for all peoples. When this expectation was not met with poor and minority peoples, blame was placed on the client. The rationale was, in Inclan's words, that "they were not verbal, motivated, insightful or able to delay gratification" (p. 332). A more effective theory for Puerto Ricans needs to have a different framework. Inclan recommends therapies that emphasize the here and now and the concrete, instead of an abstract and future orientation. The therapeutic modalities need to value the lineal family group and an understanding of the role of hierarchies in effecting change. Montijo (1985) emphasizes the importance of considering social class values when determining a therapeutic orientation for treating working-class Puerto Ricans. The goal of treatment should be to promote clients' awareness (*conciencia*) of oppression "so that they may fight more effectively for their personal and collective liberation" (p. 436).

Other studies have sought to discover problems unique to Puerto Ricans in order to develop appropriate treatment modalities. For example, Dongin, Salazar, and Cruz (1987, p. 293) identify specific culture-related difficulties they found among patients in a Hispanic treatment program:

(1) Patients had cultural conflicts as well as a need to explore cultural values, practices, and beliefs to enhance their functioning and well-being.
(2) Patients had racial and ethnic misconceptions.
(3) Patients had cultural beliefs that they could not express for fear others would not understand or would ridicule them.
(4) Patients had distorted views of the macho image and of the "submissive" female role.
(5) Patients related in Spanish only or did not understand English.

A multiethnic curriculum has value for all student populations. Such a curriculum helps all students understand their own cultures better, and also provides knowledge about other ethnic groups and their contributions. A desired outcome of such a curriculum is to help students function effectively with people from a range of cultures.

One method that offers promise with Puerto Rican adolescents is the use of folk hero modeling (Costantino, Malgady, & Rogler, 1988). This method was developed from the use of *cuentos* or folktales as a storytelling technique. In the folk hero modeling technique, stories about heroes and heroines are used to help students gain self-confidence, pride in being Puerto Rican, vocational information, coping strategies, and interest in Puerto Rican culture. Folk hero anecdotes, in both English and Spanish, have been found to produce changes in the group dynamics of participants.

It behooves educators and counselors to assist in building cultural bridges between the Puerto Rican-American culture and the dominant culture. One of the most useful tools in such an endeavor is education. Education for Puerto Rican Americans should be bilingual, because the Spanish language is of great importance to them.

The critical issues of the future for Puerto Rican Americans remain those of employment, housing, child care, and medical care. Education and local community development initiatives may be effective only if adequate support and resources are available from the dominant culture.

Questions for Review and Reflection

(1) What effect, if any, does the fact that Puerto Ricans came to the mainland United States as citizens have on their cultural practices?

(2) What role does *dignidad* play in interactions between Puerto Ricans and educators or counselors? How can this concept be used to facilitate relationships between Puerto Ricans and helpers?

(3) How can educators or counselors promote bilingualism for Puerto Ricans so that their native culture can be preserved?

(4) Why is the issue of skin color an important one among Puerto Ricans? How can knowledge of the skin color issue help educators or counselors who work with Puerto Ricans?

(5) Why should or should not Puerto Rico become a state of the United States?

(6) What role do *compadres* serve in the Puerto Rican family? How can educators or counselors use the extended family in working with Puerto Rican students or clients?

(7) There is some evidence that traditional roles are shifting among Puerto Ricans. How can knowledge of these shifts help educators or counselors who are working with Puerto Rican students or clients?

(8) How does the concept of "personalism" in the Puerto Rican culture differ from the focus on the individual in the dominant culture of the United States?

(9) Why are the therapies recommended by Inclan (1985) desirable when working with Puerto Rican clients?

(10) What must educators and counselors understand about the "macho males" and "submissive females" in the Puerto Rican culture?

References

Banks, J. A. (1987). *Teaching strategies for ethnic studies.* Boston: Allyn & Bacon.

Cardona, L. A. (1974). *The coming of the Puerto Ricans.* Mesa, AZ: Caretta.

Chenault, L. R. (1970). *The Puerto Rican migrant in New York City.* New York: Russel & Russel.

Cordasco, F. (1973). *The Puerto Rican experience: A sociological sourcebook.* Totowa, NJ: Littlefield, Adams.

Costantino, G., Malgady, R. G., & Rogler, L. H. (1988). Folk hero modeling therapy for Puerto Rican adolescents. *Journal of Adolescence, 11,* 155-165.

Dongin, D. L., Salazar, A., & Cruz, S. (1987). The Hispanic treatment program: Principles of effective psychotherapy. *Journal of Contemporary Psychotherapy, 17,* 285-295.

Fitzpatrick, J. P. (1987). *Puerto Rican Americans: The meaning of migration to the mainland.* Englewood Cliffs, NJ: Prentice-Hall.

Inclan, J. (1985). Variations in value orientations in mental health work with Puerto Ricans. *Psychotherapy, 22,* 324-334.

Juarez, R. (1985). Core issues in psychotherapy with the Hispanic child. *Psychotherapy, 22,* 441-449.

Lopez, A., & Petras, H. (1974). *Puerto Rico and the Puerto Ricans.* New York: John Wiley.

Montijo, J. A. (1985). Therapeutic relationships with the poor: A Puerto Rican perspective. *Psychotherapy, 22,* 436-441.

Quero-Chiesa, L. (1974). The anguish of the expatriate writer. In E. Mapp (Ed.), *Puerto Rican perspectives.* Metuchen, NJ: Scarecrow.

Rodriguez, C. (1989). *Puerto Ricans born in the USA.* Winchester, MA: Unwin Hyman.

Rosado, J. W. (1986). Toward an interfacing of Hispanic cultural variables with school psychology service delivery systems. *Clinical Psychology: Research and Practice, 17,* 191-199.

Simpson, G. E., & Yinger, J. M. (1972). *Racial and cultural minorities.* New York: Harper & Row.

Sociological Resources for the Social Studies. (1974). *Population change: A case study of Puerto Rico.* Boston: Allyn & Bacon.

Stevens-Arroyo, A. M. (1974). Religion and the Puerto Ricans in New York. In E. Mapp (Ed.), *Puerto Rican perspectives.* Metuchen, NJ: Scarecrow.

U.S. Department of Commerce, Bureau of the Census. (1980). *Persons of Spanish ancestry* (Suppl. report). Washington, DC: Government Printing Office.

Vice, C. (1974). The Puerto Rican woman in business. In E. Mapp (Ed.), *Puerto Rican perspectives.* Metuchen, NJ: Scarecrow.

Wagenheim, K. (1975). *A survey of Puerto Ricans on the U.S. mainland in the 1970's.* New York: Praeger.

Epilogue

Increased knowledge of multicultural issues contributes to better relationships between counselors and educators and their students and clients. This epilogue provides a summary of themes and issues that emerge from the model of multicultural understanding presented in this volume and the model's application to specific population groups. The model is designed to serve as a framework for gaining information on diverse ethnic groups so that those working with students or clients from these groups might have increased personal awareness and information about individuals and the groups in general. The model has potential usefulness in teaching, individual counseling, family counseling, group counseling, and other interventions with diverse populations.

Principles of Multicultural Practice

A number of principles serve as the guiding philosophy for the model of multicultural understanding. These are discussed in turn below.

1. Culturally diverse individuals and groups should be the primary source of information about their situation, condition, or direction. Any efforts directed at identifying, developing, or evaluating information related to the culturally diverse should involve individuals from the specific populations,

preferably in leadership roles. When teaching or counseling individuals from diverse ethnic groups, helping professionals should include strategies appropriate to those groups. These strategies should take into account both the historical and the contemporary status of the groups.

2. Multiculturalism encourages the treatment of culturally diverse group members with dignity, respect, and responsibility. Individuals from diverse ethnic groups should be treated with the same dignity and respect that any individual receives in the particular setting. Educators and counselors need to bear in mind that ethnically diverse status does not diminish or eliminate the responsibility of the individual client for meeting his or her own needs. The needs may be met within a different structural framework than might be used by a member of the dominant culture or by a member of another ethnic group, but the responsibility remains with the individual.

3. Ethnically diverse populations are heterogeneous. Any knowledge gained about members of a particular group must be balanced with the view that each person is also a unique individual, different from any other individual. Individual dimensions of behavior exist within culturally diverse groups. What might be viewed as a particular style or pattern for the ethnically diverse group may not represent a specific style or pattern for any given individual within the group. Counselors and educators are encouraged to keep in mind that students or clients from ethnically diverse populations bring with them many beliefs, values, and attitudes that result from membership in their ethnic group. The manner in which these beliefs, values, and attitudes are expressed is influenced by an individually unique adaptation based on personal style.

4. Educational institutions should have well-defined policy statements and curricula regarding the significance, purpose, and thrust of their multicultural efforts. The multicultural focus should be a part of the core of what is done in any setting, rather than peripheral in nature. In far too many cases, attention to multicultural issues is an afterthought rather than a part of the foundation of program efforts, as it should be. Multiculturalism is not simply the addition of content about ethnically diverse peoples; it involves rethinking the policies related to the use of all material in a curriculum.

Individuals interested in moving toward a multicultural program should begin by (a) recognizing that education and/or counseling are not value-free; (b) identifying current biases and deficiencies in the existing program, by conducting a critique of the environment; (c) acquiring a thorough knowledge of the philosophy and theory concerning multiculturalism and its application to the specific setting; (d) acquiring, evaluating, adapting, and developing materials appropriate to the multicultural effort being undertaken;

and (e) determining an effective means of involving members of the ethnically diverse population(s) in the effort to make the program responsive to all persons served. These preparatory efforts should lead to a solid foundation upon which to build a multicultural program that is reasonably sensitive to the needs of the various populations served.

5. Multicultural efforts must focus on normal behaviors and wellness, rather than on abnormal behaviors and illness. Far too many efforts at meeting the needs of ethnically diverse individuals fail because they begin from a viewpoint of abnormality rather than normality. Factors such as "low self-esteem" and "self-hatred" are frequently assumed to be characteristic of ethnically diverse group members without any investigation of the basis on which such claims are made. We must also use care in how we translate research results and generalize them to populations larger than those used in the research investigations.

6. Multiculturalism requires that educators and counselors be aware of the systemic dimensions of racism and alienation, and thereby attempt to understand the experiences, life-styles, and values of students and clients. As convenient as it might be to pretend that racism does not permeate most of the culture of the United States, we must be aware of it, how it affects members of the dominant culture, and how it affects members of ethnically diverse cultural groups. If schools and other institutions are to be successful with all students and clients, there must be acknowledgment of the prevailing values in the system. Because awareness is the initial step in dealing with any problem, representatives of institutions and members of culturally diverse populations must understand how racism affects both groups.

7. Educators and counselors must be trained who are capable of demonstrating effectiveness with individuals from culturally diverse ethnic groups. Training programs must be expanded beyond single course offerings into areas that deal directly with the needs of culturally diverse populations. Training must move beyond rhetoric about cultural pluralism to what is real in the lives of the culturally diverse. Programs should focus on training counselors and educators for roles as change agents who will challenge the system rather than modify the behavior of culturally diverse students or clients to fit the system.

General Guidelines to
Enhance Multicultural Understanding

These guidelines, adapted from Locke (1989), are presented here to extend what teachers and counselors use from either the model of multicultural understanding or the information on a specific culturally diverse group.

1. Learn as much as possible about your own culture. One can appreciate another culture much more if one first has an appreciation of one's own.

2. Work at being open and honest in your relationships with culturally diverse populations. Leave yourself open to different attitudes and values and encourage those different from yourself to be open and honest with you about issues related to their cultures. Attend to the verbal and nonverbal communication patterns between yourself and your culturally diverse students or clients.

3. Seek to develop genuine respect and appreciation of culturally diverse attitudes and behaviors. Demonstrate that you both recognize and value the cultures of those different from yourself. Respect can be demonstrated by starting with the life experiences of the student or client, and not the experiences of the teacher or counselor.

4. Take advantage of all available opportunities to participate in activities in the communities of culturally different groups.

5. Keep in mind that individuals from culturally diverse groups are both members of their groups and unique individuals as well. Strive to keep a healthy balance between your view of students or clients as cultural beings and as unique beings.

6. Learn to examine cultural biases, prejudices, and stereotypes. Eliminate all of your behaviors that suggest prejudice or racism and do not tolerate such behaviors in your colleagues or in other members of your own cultural group. Teach your students or clients how to recognize bias and how to challenge stereotypes.

7. Encourage administrators and/or supervisors in your school or agency to institutionalize practices that acknowledge the diversity among your students or clients.

8. Hold high expectations of culturally diverse students or clients and encourage others who work with diverse populations to do likewise.

9. Ask questions about the cultures of ethnically diverse groups. Learn as much as possible about different cultures and share what you learn with others.

10. Develop culturally specific strategies, techniques, and programs to foster the psychological development of culturally different individuals and groups.

A Vision

In 1972, the Commission on Multicultural Education of the American Association of Colleges of Teacher Education (AACTE) issued a statement titled "No One Model American." The document states that multiculturalism "recognizes cultural diversity as a fact of life in American society, and it affirms that this cultural diversity is a valuable resource that should be preserved and extended" (see AACTE, 1973, p. 264).

This statement communicates a vision of a better society, one that is possible if the current efforts to create a truly multicultural outlook are implemented and sustained. It recognizes the multicultural and pluralistic nature of U.S. society and calls for the development of comprehensive approaches to meeting the needs of all students and clients. To make a difference, we must continue theory development relevant to the culturally diverse, conduct quantitative and qualitative research on diverse populations, and ensure that curriculum offerings are inclusive of all groups within this society.

There is a great need for new and different models for working with culturally diverse populations in the United States. The United States is a richer nation as a result of the many different cultures that have contributed, and continue to contribute, to making the country what it is. We need to be aware of the many values that culturally diverse groups add to the quality, vitality, and strength of the nation. We also need to be aware of the differences that exist among our culturally diverse populations.

The differences that exist between members of the dominant culture and members of ethnically diverse cultures are real. Many of these differences are grounded in the cultures from which individuals form their worldviews. Others are the result of unique differences between individuals regardless of cultural background. Counselors and educators must be aware of these differences and the ways in which these differences complicate interactions between themselves and their students and clients. The ideas discussed here may be useful toward that end.

References

American Association of Colleges of Teacher Education (AACTE). (1973, Winter). No one model American. *Journal of Teacher Education, 24,* 264-265.

Locke, D. C. (1989). Fostering the self-esteem of African-American children. *Elementary School Guidance and Counseling, 23,* 254-259.

Index

About the Author

Don C. Locke is Professor and Head of the Department of Counselor Education at North Carolina State University in Raleigh. He began his career as a high school social studies teacher in Fort Wayne, Indiana, where he also worked as a high school counselor for two years. He earned his doctorate at Ball State University in 1974. He has been active in state, regional, and national counseling organizations, and has served as President of the North Carolina Association for Counseling and Development, as Chair of the Southern Region Branch of the American Association for Counseling and Development (AACD), and as Secretary of the Association for Counselor Education and Supervision (ACES). He has also been a member of the ACES Editorial Board, President of the Southern Association for Counselor Education and Supervision (SACES), and a member of the AACD Governing Council. The author or coauthor of more than 50 publications, he is currently focusing on multicultural issues.